Judy Redmond

1979

FLOWER ARRANGING
FROM
YOUR GARDEN

FLOWER ARRANGING
FROM
YOUR GARDEN

Sheila Macqueen

Chilton Book Company
Radnor, Pennsylvania

Acknowledgments

I would like to thank Patricia Herrmann for much kind and valuable help and also Roy Hay for contributing such excellent horticultural advice. My thanks go also to Roy T. Smith and Bill Haines of Studio 189 for taking such beautiful photographs and for their enthusiasm and good humour on many arduous photography days. The black and white photographs are reproduced by permission of the Harry Smith Photographic Collection.

Finally, I am most grateful to Ward Lock and their staff, who could not have been more helpful and welcoming and I am delighted that this, the fourth book Peter Crawley has asked me to write, should appear under his own Hyperion Books imprint. With understanding and kindness he has given me all the encouragement I could possibly have wished for.

Sheila Macqueen

Contents

Foreword

To anyone who has had the pleasure of observing Sheila Macqueen in action during one of her flower arranging demonstrations, or of strolling through her garden, this book comes as no surprise. It has been my privilege to enjoy both these experiences, the essence of which she has crystallized within these pages.

Her genuine love and respect for all growing plants is very evident, and there is contagion in her enthusiasm for creating beauty through flowers, either indoors or out. Her many years of practical training form a firm foundation for her artistry, but it is in her own garden that one is most aware of her intense horticultural interest. Perhaps this has been born of necessity in order to have at hand the exact forms and color required at all seasons, but whatever the motive the result has been a happy marriage of both her talents, each enhancing the other.

Far from a stranger to the American public, she has been well known here for many years through her talks to garden clubs, horticulturists, church groups, etc. all across the country, as she gaily criss-crosses this broad land as though it were no larger than her native England. Repeat engagements bear witness to her success, and she always manages to create something new and inspiring, always presented with charm, taste, and subtle humor. Her remarkable abilities as a teacher have been recognized in the recent award of the Garden Club of America medal for education in the field of flower arrangement.

Her delightful personality, her sincere love for her vocation, her artistry, sense of color, and elegant grace come through in print as well as on stage. Also in these pages we can walk through her garden and share many valuable growing hints. Through her countless visits to most areas of this country Sheila has gained a sympathetic understanding of our climatic problems and variations. The cultural notes by one as expert as Roy Hay strengthen the usefulness of the book and add a practical extra dimension.

Meeting her at the airport is always an exciting adventure, for inevitably she is trailing an enormous plastic bag bursting with left-over material: fascinating bits of foliage, odd-shaped branches, brilliant blossoms, salvaged from preceding lectures and ready to be re-cycled with imagination and style. You may be sure that any extras from whatever you have provided will go travelling off in the same way to her next destination! A drive with her along a country road, a city park, or a walk around one's own limited property always produces surprises as her perceptive eye spots unusual coloured foliage, graceful tendril, or unassuming weed, which through her magic touch can produce a masterpiece. Not that she scorns the ubiquitous 'florists' dozen', but infinitely prefers the fun and challenge of scavenging and invention.

Just as it is a joy to welcome Sheila Macqueen herself into our homes and hearts, it is equally so to welcome her book to this country. For her American audience I feel sure it will open new doors to pleasure and insight in the boundless world of plants and flowers.

Elizabeth P. Corning
Former President, Garden Club of America
Albany, New York

Introduction

You may well wonder whether there is anything new to be said about flower arranging. For a long time I have wanted to write a book about plants that are of equal value to the gardener and the flower arranger, as to me there is really no greater pleasure than arranging a vase of flowers and foliage that I have grown in my own garden. It is something that I have been learning about for many years, and I dearly hope that my experience can help you.

I have always said that I started to grow flowers so that I could pick and arrange them, but suddenly found I could hardly bear to cut what I had grown. At this point I think perhaps I started to become a gardener. Real gardeners always prefer to see the plants growing, but I feel this limits the enjoyment one gets from them. A lovely display of flowers in the house will be appreciated by a great number of people, whereas, on a wet evening for instance, only the real gardening enthusiasts will venture out with you to inspect one small flower that you may have grown from seed and nurtured for years. So, although I love my garden, I have continued to pick from it, but with respect for the plants, learning how long each takes to grow and how to avoid ruining the shape by thoughtless cutting.

In this book I have tried to take you through all the stages from filling the bare earth to putting the last touches to a flower arrangement; and I have also attempted to deal with some of the pitfalls that you may encounter. For instance, in starting a new garden—always a challenge—I personally have often made the mistake of allowing too little space for my plants: perhaps I never expected them to survive and grow really big. So in giving you some suggestions for designing a small garden, I have included plants for quick results that could be eliminated at a later date, and also ideas for dealing with an overgrown garden where one must be ruthless.

Talking about cultivation is not easy, especially as I wanted to include helpful notes for US readers too. I know that in many areas of America, gardening can be a heartbreaking occupation, with cold, cold winters and burning summers; and even in my own English village I have had difficulty in growing a plant that flourishes almost next door. In spite of the problems, however, there are many plants that will do well if you are willing to give time and care to the garden, and I feel sure the results will reward you a thousandfold.

My gardening knowledge is very limited, so I have been particularly lucky to have the help of Roy Hay who has not only written the chapter on planting, growing and propagation in general, but has supplied all the correct cultivation notes for each plant listed in the main section of the book.

It is naturally very difficult to select a list of plants suitable for both gardening and flower arranging when there is so much to choose from. The particular species and varieties I have included are purely my own choice, but I would like to think I have not missed too many of your favourites. I have tried to concentrate on plants that are comparatively easy to grow, are useful for their foliage or for the scent, shape or colour of their flowers, and which also last well in water; so my list really does cover a very wide field.

My aim has always been to achieve good colour in the garden all the year round, and at the same time have something to pick, so that growing and arranging can give you equal pleasure.

7

Ideas for a
Flower Arranger's Garden

When planning a garden from scratch, the layout is the most important part. If you have lots of time, and it is financially feasible, it is best to start by clearing the area completely of stones, weeds and rough grass, using a rotary cultivator or, if the weeds are really vicious, applying simazine (though I would only advise this if the plot is full of something like ground elder, as the soil has to be rested for nine months after treatment). Every day spent in preparation at this early stage will save a year in the future, but the first objective of this initial clearing is to let you see the basic shape of the ground and any noticeable features in or near it.

Now you are ready to make your plan. Start from *inside* your house and walk from room to room, deciding which room you will be sitting in most, and go to the window in that room from which you get the best view of the garden. If you really feel you will not see very much from the house, decide on the sitting area you will use most outside. Then take paper and pencil and make rough sketches of what you would like to see from these positions. I know most books will tell you to start with a layout on graph paper, but I feel this comes later, for after all you don't look down on trees, paths and lawns and I think it is important to try first of all to visualize your garden as you will eventually see it. Study the problems, such as an ugly shed to be hidden, or a cold prevailing wind, draw in the features you want to emphasize, such as a fine tree or a natural slope, and remember practical considerations. Ask all your friends for advice: everyone loves to give advice, though you may not want to take it all; often you will find that something will strike one person and something else another, and you will be given quite a lot of useful ideas. I well remember that once when we decided to make a pathway between the house and a wall, someone said so sensibly 'Make it wide enough for the barrow'. Thank goodness we did; we saved ourselves a lot of walking.

I shall not attempt to advise you on every aspect of garden design, but here are a number of practical points you should try to remember:

The cost of upkeep and the time you can spend on your garden should always be borne in mind. Grass paths, for instance, look attractive, but make for a lot of work and, especially in the vegetable garden, some form of concrete or stone path will save effort in the future.

When you are thinking about your lawn, remember that bold sweeping curves not only look better, but will save you hours of manoeuvring the mower around fiddly corners.

Never plant a flower border too near a hedge: make a path at the back, which makes for easy working and prevents weeds from beyond and under the hedge from encroaching into your garden.

Always make borders wider than you think they should be, and try to place at least some so that you can look along them: you can get a wonderful effect from a wide flower border, whereas narrow borders seen straight on are rather disappointing.

9

Avoid too many small flower beds: they look fussy and need lots of attention.

A paved area can be a lovely feature in a garden, with either sink gardens or just paving and sweet-smelling plants such as pinks, lavender and honeysuckle. Best of all, if you can design your paved area so that it is close by the house, slightly sunken or sheltered by wall and hedge, you have a perfect 'sitting-out' place.

Rock gardens also need to be near the house to my way of thinking. The whole pattern of our lives has changed: when there were gardeners it was pleasant to wander round a garden and enjoy one surprise after another, walking from hedged rose garden to lily pool to rock garden; now I feel envy for those of my friends who had the foresight to place a rock pool or rock garden as a feature easily seen from the house or perhaps next to the sun loggia. Even on a chill spring evening or wet summer night, you can then sit and enjoy the garden: with a bit of clever lighting and maybe a drink in your hand, what could make the view more attractive! The Americans are past masters at this, and I have sat in some of the smallest gardens, where lovely walls festooned with colourful plants and hidden lighting make you feel they are twice or three times the size they really are.

If you have to tackle an overgrown garden, in some ways it can be more difficult; but at least there will be some trees or shrubs that will give the garden a furnished look, and this does help. Try not to dash in with a bulldozer and make a clean sweep until you have had a chance to see the garden right through one season. So often there are hidden treasures that can easily be destroyed, never to be found again. If you live with the garden for a year, you may find that there is a good reason for some of the earlier planting. In a garden near me, for instance, the new owner cut down all the polygonum or knotweed, covering a fence, only to find it had covered the most unsightly and makeshift structure, which of course was exactly why it had been put there in the first place. I had an old plum tree cut down when we first moved in, but it was not until the following autumn that I bitterly regretted it; as soon as all the leaves were off the other trees, I had an uninterrupted view of the next-door neighbour's house, and pleasant as it is, I would really much have preferred the old tree. These are just two warnings against being over hasty. The first year will not be wasted; whilst you are thinking about ways and means of re-planning the parts you find unattractive, the better sections can be improved. Laurel and rhododendrons, for instance, are shrubs that can stand being cut back really hard, allowing new growth to appear which is often such an improvement. Don't do all your pruning at once, however: do it a little at a time or maybe cut back every other one. I know exactly what can happen when a man has a saw or pruners in his hands: it's a case of a clean sweep regardless, but this may have the effect of killing, not curing overgrown shrubs.

Whether your garden is one you have created yourself or one you have taken over, it is a good idea occasionally to ask someone else to look at it with a fresh eye. A great friend who is an excellent gardener came to help me once, and every now and then would say something like 'Why do you keep that old rose when it never really does anything?' How right she was, but somehow I had never thought of getting rid of it and replacing it with a more attractive plant. This can often happen and is just one way in which you can improve your garden.

When you have decided on the basic layout, it is time to get out the squared paper and think about the plants you want. Don't attempt to complete the work in one season. I find it best to have a five-year plan and work outwards, concentrating first on the area near the house. If you are lucky enough to have a pleasant view, at first you need do no more than plant for a little colour and flowers to pick, but even in later years, remember not to interrupt the view.

One of the loveliest gardens I know is in Middleburg, Virginia, in the United States, where two vast borders sweep towards the foothills of the Blue Mountains. Beautifully planted with a background of good shrubs, cleverly interspersed with evergreens, were huge clumps of peonies and iris. This kind of treatment can be used for even the smallest garden: planting to create a view, or frame an existing one, using shrubs in the herbaceous border to save work, placing evergreens to give winter life and summer contrast, and planting in clumps to create a simple restful effect. It is the same technique in the garden as for flower arranging, grouping for contrast and allowing leaves to play a major part in both cases. When arranging a vase, the best way to avoid a spotty effect is to place together one or two flowers of the same colour. For example, an outline of a twiggy flowering shrub such as forsythia, then some pieces of the green hellebore with delicate but solid heads, a centre focal point of two rounded heads of *Petasites japonicus*, or three or five yellow tulips with a few stems of straw hyacinth on either side. Exactly the same principles can be followed when you plan your border: in this case the forsythia and large-leaved petasites would be at the back, with the smaller plants in front providing different leaf forms and colour. Or try putting three golden-leaved hosta together with three green-leaved ones, with dark-leaved bergenia or tellima next to the gold hosta, then maybe a russet leucothoë or two, and behind them a clump of grey artichoke and grey onopordum thistle together with a greyish-leaved eucalyptus. To contrast with the grey mass, you can have a pink or yellow-flowering rhododendron, then two clumps of euphorbia as another contrast in leaf form but with a colour to blend with the hosta in front of it. Try to put together plants that set each other off and look well together even when not in flower. My favourite green hellebores, for example, look so well in the early spring against an evergreen hedge or under the bare twigs of *Cornus mas*. The lime green of *Alchemilla mollis* can be used to set off *Alstroemeria ligtu* hybrids both in vase and in border.

It is also fun to work out nice ideas for underplanting, but this is much more a matter of trial and error: I did try polyanthus under forsythia, but have never yet had the luck to find them all in flower at the same time. And only after twenty-odd years have I succeeded in getting my hardy cyclamen to flower well under a silver birch. However, this should not stop you from trying out ideas, for it is amazing how quickly the years fly by.

One big problem when deciding on plants to grow is that, having spent so much on your house—usually more than one ever intended—there seems to be little left for the garden. So you may feel that you want to grow most things yourself and many from seed. Do bear in mind how long this will take, though, and invest in a few large shrubs and trees and some of the plants that will take longest to grow, such as peonies, roses, hellebores, alchemilla, onopordum, *Alstroemeria ligtu* hybrids, euphorbias, hostas, delphinium and a few plants for the rock garden. Hopefully, many of your gardener friends will have spare plants and will be happy to give you seedlings and cuttings, and I do advise you to accept these even if they are not what you want, for they can always be replaced at a later date.

I tend to plant much too close together, perhaps because I never really think that anything is going to grow, but I suppose the ideal would be to plant each subject with enough space to grow. If you are strong-minded and do this, I suggest filling in during the early years with annuals, especially those like atriplex and moluccella, which are also lovely for picking and drying.

As a foil for your borders and hedges, you will of course want a good lawn. I think it is wisest to sow a lawn for the best grass, but I know that this is not always practicable. We really had no choice, for instance: a sea of clay, rough ground with nettles and indeed every conceivable weed, two very small children with nowhere to play outside—we decided very quickly that our first priority was to turf a lawn. The result has never been very good. However we put geese on another area of rough grass for a year, and with constant fertilizing and cutting it has improved out of all recognition and is undoubtedly our best piece of lawn today. In my view, frequent cutting can make a good lawn even from poor grass. In my garden I soon found that even if I worked in it for every minute I could spare during the week, it was only when my husband cut the grass over the weekend that the garden began to look well.

How difficult it is to tell anyone what to do with a piece of land! But I *can* tell you that working in the garden can give you more pleasure than many, many other things: I find that time passes more quickly than anywhere else and surely no other activity is so rewarding.

If I could choose only ten plants to grow for flower arranging, the ones I would choose, and would hate to live without, are:

Alchemilla mollis
Artichoke (*Cynara scolymus*)
Arum italicum 'Pictum'
Bergenias
Euphorbias
Hedera *english Ivy*
Hellebore *Christmas Rose*
Hosta
Phytolacca americana
Sedum

All of these may be used in arrangements for many months in the year.

Cultivation *by Roy Hay*

The most successful flower arrangers I have known have loved plants and flowers and have given as much time and thought to creating a beautiful garden as they have to creating lovely flower arrangements. Sheila Macqueen, and Constance Spry before her, has done just this.

I assume that the flower arranger who wishes to grow as many plants as her garden can accommodate also wishes to spend as little time and labour on them as possible. So in the pages that follow I have tried to suggest ways of cutting the corners and minimizing the man/woman hours needed to cope with the garden maintenance.

Of course, the larger the garden, the easier it is to produce material for flower arranging without affecting the general attractiveness of the garden as a whole. In the palmy days before the wars a garden designed, say, by Gertrude Jekyll would have a 'cutting garden' hard by the entrance to the domestic quarters. Today, in all but the smallest gardens, it is still possible to have an area, usually a part of the vegetable plot, where some plants are grown expressly for cutting. Here one can have daffodils, tulips and wallflowers for the spring; followed by, say, sweet-williams, Dutch, English or Spanish irises to flower in June before the main summer flowers are ready. Then come peonies and pyrethrums, pinks and *Scabiosa caucasica*. These are followed by gladioli, early chrysanthemums, and dahlias. Also in the cutting garden we can have a few plants of everlastings like helichrysums, statice, and Chinese lanterns (physalis).

A cutting garden need not be very large because one can pack quite a lot of plants into quite a small area. Tulips, daffodils and Dutch irises may be planted 6 in (15 cm) apart each way in blocks of say 4 ft (1·2 m) square. Or they may be planted in blocks of a convenient width for covering with cloches, of which there are many different shapes and sizes now available. These normally consist of moulded semi-rigid plastic or thin plastic sheeting, supported by some type of wire frame.

As with garden produce generally, it is out-of-season crops—early or late, that are most appreciated, as they come in when the shop article is at its most expensive. Gladioli too may be planted fairly close together—6 in (15 cm) apart in rows 12–15 in (30–38 cm) apart.

If you grow vegetables, then gladioli, outdoor chrysanthemums, dahlias, sweet peas, and other annual flowers are very useful to work into the three- or four-year rotation. Only too often in a small garden and for a small family one does not grow a wide enough selection of vegetables to ensure that, say, cabbages or peas do not have to be grown too frequently on the same spot. The flowers will help to ring the changes and make for a better crop rotation.

Planting times. In general trees, shrubs and climbers, and herbaceous plants may be transplanted or planted at any time between October and March provided the soil is not waterlogged, frozen, or covered with snow. There are exceptions of course. Evergreens may be planted in the autumn in reasonably mild climates, but they should be in the ground in Octo-

13

ber so that they have time to make new roots while the soil is still warm. They may also need protection of hessian, plastic sheeting or the like in severe spells. Spraying with an anti-desiccant is also desirable.

Herbaceous plants with fleshy roots are best planted in autumn, while those with fibrous roots may be planted either in autumn or spring. They may even be planted as late as April, provided attention is paid to watering until they are well established.

Most bulbs or corms are planted in the autumn, but some, such as lilies, gladioli and nerines are planted in spring, and colchicums in late summer.

Container-grown plants—trees, shrubs and climbers, and herbaceous plants, may theoretically be planted at any time when the ground is workable. But if planted in the spring, they will need to be carefully watched and generously watered in dry spells.

Soil preparation. Soils vary enormously and all need thorough cultivation with the addition usually of organic material—well-rotted farmyard or stable manure, garden compost, hop manure, or even peat and bonemeal. This is partly to improve the moisture-holding capacity of the lighter soils, or to improve the texture of heavier soils, to encourage rapid root action— also, of course, to supply plant food.

Many of our most beautiful plants—rhododendrons, azaleas and camellias for example— must have acid soil. It is possible, however, to grow them on alkaline or chalky soils by taking out a hole about 2–2½ ft (60–75 cm) deep and about 3 ft (1 m) square, and lining this with plastic sheeting. Then the hole is filled with peat and the plants fed regularly with a suitable fertilizer. Alternatively, one can make a raised bed, say 2–2½ ft (60–75 cm) above the ground, casing this round with flat stone or brick walls, lengths of timber, logs or even old railway sleepers, or tie bars as they are called in the United States. These beds are then filled with peat as suggested above. If one simply digs a hole and fills it with peat, in a year or so the limy water will seep in from the sides and the shrubs will not thrive.

When planting trees and shrubs generally, there is the temptation to skimp the preparation and just dig out a hole large enough to take the root ball. It is better to dig over a larger area— say 2–3 square ft (about 60–90 sq cm), so that the shrub or tree can quickly make a new root system. This is especially desirable on heavy soils, because if one just takes out a small hole, it may act like a sump and water may collect in it and cause actual drowning of the roots.

I like to use plenty of moist peat mixed with bonemeal when planting trees or shrubs. Use a double handful of bonemeal to a 2 gallon (9 l) bucket of peat, well mixed. After forking over and working in whatever organic material is available, take out a hole amply large enough for the roots to be spread out to their full extent, and loosen the bottom of the hole to a fork's depth.

If the tree needs a stake, insert this next, and then spread 1–2 in (about 4 cm) of the peat and bonemeal mixture over the bottom. Place the tree or shrub against the stake, and cover the roots with a 2 in (5 cm) layer of the peat. Add soil and some more peat, lift the tree up and down gently a few times to settle the soil among the roots, and firm with the feet as the filling of the hole proceeds. Leave a shallow, saucer-like depression on the surface of the soil around the plant to facilitate watering should this be necessary in the first summer after planting.

Thorough preparation of the soil is also desirable for herbaceous plants, bulbs, and plants from seed, although it is neither necessary nor wise to make the ground too rich for annual flowers as they may make too much foliage at the expense of flowers.

There are several ways in which newly planted trees, shrubs, herbaceous plants and bulbs, may be helped to establish themselves and to make good growth in subsequent years. Obviously regular and adequate watering in dry periods which may occur at any time from spring to autumn will prevent a check to growth, and even in times of prolonged drought save the life of a recently planted tree or shrub.

It is important, however, to start watering early, before the plant has received any check or is showing signs of distress. Too often people wait until a plant begins to wilt before applying water. By then it may be too late. It may be necessary to apply water as early as April in some areas and in some seasons.

Next, too often people do not apply enough water at a time—$1\frac{1}{2}$–2 gallons (7–9 l) to the square yd (m) is not too much, and in dry weather may be required twice a week. Then a mulch or layer of some organic material spread over the soil around the plants is extremely helpful in keeping moisture in the soil, and in suppressing weeds, which of course rob our plants of water and plant food.

There are many mulching materials—well-decayed manure, half-decayed leaves, leaf-mould, peat, garden compost, sawdust, bracken, straw—all will suppress weeds and help to keep the moisture in the soil. In the United States great use is made of bark, wood chips, and corn cob husks suitably milled.

To be really useful a mulch should be about 2 in (5 cm) deep. Always see that the soil is thoroughly moist before applying the mulch. It is desirable to allow the ground to warm up in spring before applying the mulch as it will slow down the increase in soil temperature if put on too soon. Also, remember if watering becomes necessary to apply about $1\frac{1}{2}$ gallons (7 l) of water to wet the mulch first, and then apply a further $1\frac{1}{2}$–2 gallons (7–9 l) to wet the soil.

Wood wastes, such as sawdust, as well as straw, can cause a temporary shortage of nitrogen when dug into the soil or even when used as a mulch. What happens is that the soil bacteria, essential to plant life, set to work to decompose the sawdust. The bacteria need nitrogen to live and this they take from the soil. The soil gets it back in due course when the sawdust or straw is rotted down, but there may be a temporary shortage. To overcome this, such materials should be given a dressing of sulphate of ammonia. In practice I have found that a handful of sulphate of ammonia scattered over a square yd (m) of a 2 in (5 cm) thick mulch of sawdust is adequate.

The practice of applying an anti-desiccant spray to evergreen shrubs and other plants at planting time, and again say two or three months later, is now becoming very popular. These water-borne plastic sprays greatly reduce water loss by transpiration from the leaves and thus prevent shrivelling and possible death of the plants. These anti-desiccants, of course, we use to spray Christmas trees to prevent needle drop, and our holly and ivy decorations to prevent premature shrivelling.

In addition to the plant foods that may have been worked into the soil at planting time, foliar feeds—fertilizers sprayed on to the leaves of plants—can greatly increase root development. This is especially valuable in dry summers because, obviously, a plant with a greater root system is in a stronger position to draw up water and food. All plants benefit from foliar or leaf feeding but spraying the foliage should not be commenced before mid-April; thereafter the feed should be applied at 10 to 14 day intervals, three or four times.

In any garden weed control is a problem, and can take up a good deal of time. Fortunately we have new chemicals to help us with our war on weeds, but the age-old methods are still valid. Mulching, as I have already pointed out, provided the ground is free from weeds before the mulch is applied, can work wonders. Of course, there will always be some weeds on a mulched surface, from wind- or bird-borne seeds, but these are easily pulled out.

Then, as the old adage has it, 'If you hoe when there are no weeds, there never will be any weeds'. Easy to say, not so easy to carry out, because there are wet periods when it is not feasible to go and hoe, or there are times when one is just not available to do the hoeing. But if one can just lightly riffle through the top $\frac{1}{2}$ in (1 cm) of soil when the weeds are very tiny, the work is easy and does not take long. It is when the weeds have been allowed to get a deep root hold and have to be chopped off, raked up and carted to the compost heap that weed control becomes a weary chore.

But chemical weed control saves much time and energy. Most gardeners are familiar with selective weedkillers to control weeds on lawns. They will also deal with weeds such as ground elder and convolvulus among shrubs, although more than one application may be necessary.

There are also total weedkillers such as simazine, which will control weeds on paths and drives for a whole growing season if applied in late winter.

But the most valuable weedkillers, as far as saving of time and labour is concerned, are paraquat and the residual weedkillers. Paraquat is a total weedkiller—it will kill every living plant it comes into contact with, but it does not affect the soil. One can destroy a crop of weeds on the ground, hoe it over and sow seeds immediately. In warm weather it will cause weeds to wither and die in 36 hours. It is most effective if applied when the weeds are very small. Once they are well rooted, more than one application may be required to kill them.

The residual weedkillers are quite remarkable and splendid labour savers. Gardeners are only slowly realizing how valuable they are. Briefly, they keep clean ground clean. They destroy seedling weeds a few hours after they have germinated. They have no effect on established cultivated plants. They come in granular and in liquid form. Applied to clean ground from April onwards they will keep it clean for up to 12 or 14 weeks. These weedkillers are among the greatest contributions to labour saving in the garden ever made since the invention of the mowing machine.

We do not make nearly enough use in Britain of what I call the 'third dimension'—that is, growing plants up walls or fences, posts, porches or pergolas. So many lovely plants, useful for flower arrangers, can be grown in this way.

Nowadays there are easy methods of training roses, honeysuckles, clematis and other plants against a wall or fence. The easiest is to fix square-meshed, plastic-covered wire panels to the wall. If 6 in (15 cm) vine eyes, or nails, are driven into the walls or fence, the panels can be wired to them leaving a gap of 3–4 in (around 9 cm) between the panels and the wall. The beauty of these panels is that one can push new shoots in and out of the meshes as they grow, and there is no need to tie them in place.

One can also buy rolls of pure plastic square-meshed panels which can be stretched against walls or fences, or wound round stout poles or pergola posts. Again, it is so simple to train shoots of climbing plants in and out of the square meshes.

Still on the subject of labour saving, let us consider ground-covering plants. There are many that can be useful to the flower arranger, such as pachysandra, tiarella, ivies, bergenia, periwinkle and others. They are effective weed smotherers, and once established need no further attention. But it is essential to have the ground into which these plants are to be planted absolutely free of weeds. They take one, or maybe two, seasons to spread and cover their allotted area and in the meantime weed seeds will germinate and the seedlings will have to be hoed off. But, as described above, a residual weedkiller applied two or three times during the summer should take care of these weeds. Naturally this method of controlling weeds works extremely well in beds or borders of herbaceous plants, and in a rock garden.

Opposite
Outside Sheila Macqueen's 400-year-old Hertfordshire cottage in summer.

In the United States great use is made of ivy, varieties of hedera, for ground cover, and indeed much more use of this splendid genus could be made for this purpose in British gardens. Ivies will grow under trees, and when the tree leaves fall upon them it is only necessary to switch them back and forth with a broom so that they fall beneath the ivy foliage. There they will in due course rot down and nourish the ivy plants. Of course, one does have to see that the ivies do not start to climb the trees. While ivy is suitable for ground cover in shade, it is also very useful in full sun.

Thinking still about labour saving, there is the question of herbaceous borders against a wall or fence as opposed to free-standing beds. For many years it has been assumed that a herbaceous border must have a 'background'—a hedge, a wall, or a fence. Very nice such borders are, but the plants tend to reach towards the light and become 'drawn' or more lanky than they would be if grown in a free-standing bed in an open part of the garden. Many plants that would not need staking in a free-standing bed have to be supported in a border against a wall or hedge.

So I would suggest to gardening flower arrangers that they move borders 3–4 ft (about 1 m) away from walls or hedges, or, better still, if space permits, grow their herbaceous plants in free-standing beds in the open parts of the garden.

These beds should be not more than 4 ft (1·2 m) wide so that you can reach into them easily from each side for hoeing, staking, or for cutting the flowers and removing dead heads.

There is yet another advantage of the free-standing bed. Some plants often do best if given a little shade from the heat of the midday sun. One can create some shade by planting a dwarf shrub or even some taller herbaceous plants, and shade lovers may be planted on the north or north-west side of them.

Propagation. Many people who embrace gardening as a hobby, or who are inveigled into it, as it were, because they wish to have flowers or foliage that you seldom, if ever, see in the shops, are timid about trying to propagate plants. They say they are not greenfingered. Now I have always had my doubts about this 'greenfinger' myth. You hear people say that their mother, aunt, grandmother or somebody, had greenfingers: 'She just used to stick bits of plants in the ground and they grew'. But it is nearly always an old person they are referring to. Very seldom do they say my young niece or daughter has greenfingers. Successful propagation—or indeed success with growing plants generally—is bound up with a capacity to observe how plants react to given treatment, to remember what one did last year that was successful, or what was not.

Raising plants from seed is not difficult provided one follows the instructions. Always sow seeds very thinly; always thin seedlings, and remove weeds as soon as the plants are large enough to handle. Annual flowers particularly can be severely checked if they have to fight their neighbours and weed seedlings for air, sunshine, water and plant food.

Many herbaceous plants and ground-cover plants may be increased by simple division. Clumps of, say, phloxes, pyrethrums and the like, may be split up and young strong pieces with two or three shoots and a good quantity of roots may be separated and planted, either in autumn or spring. Always plant the young strong pieces from the outside of the clump, and discard the worn-out centre.

Propagation by cuttings is much easier than most newcomers to gardening believe. Many plants root readily if the cutting is taken at the right time, inserted in a suitable soil mix and

Opposite
A view of the garden in spring with polyanthus and
flowering cherries in the foreground.

given the right conditions—a frame maybe, a cloche, or a propagating case if one is more ambitious.

Many shrubs may be propagated by means of half-ripe cuttings—shoots about 3–4 in (around 9 cm) long taken during the summer. Usually they are pulled off the main stem with a 'heel'—that is, a sliver of the old wood still attached to the base. There will also be a sliver of bark which is trimmed off with a sharp knife or a razor blade. If the base of the cutting is dipped into a 'hormone' type rooting compound, either a powder or a liquid, this usually encourages and hastens rooting.

A good rooting medium is made up of about four parts of fine peat and one part of coarse sand or grit. Do not use the soft yellow builders' sand. The grit should be really coarse with pieces up to $\frac{1}{4}$ in (0·5 cm) across in it. For small quantities of cuttings, however, it is probably best to buy a bag of a cutting mix. Fill the pots with this, and insert the cuttings round the inner edge of the pot, or insert them in trays filled with the mix. One can even buy small flat plastic packs filled with a cutting mixture. These are opened up and the cuttings inserted directly therein. The pots or boxes may be placed in a cold frame or under cloches in summer, and kept moist and shaded from strong sunshine.

Shrubs such as flowering currant, weigelas, brooms, heathers, philadelphus, conifers, and many more, may be rooted from such cuttings.

Soft cuttings of such plants as hydrangeas, aucubas, choisyas, ivies, and jasmine may be rooted in the same way.

It is worth while, however, if one is really interested in propagation, to acquire a simple book on the subject, or to study the propagation section of a gardening encyclopedia in the local library. There is no more fascinating and rewarding aspect of gardening than the propagation of one's favourite plants, or the successful rooting of cuttings acquired from friends.

Another subject that puzzles and often frightens the new gardener is pruning. The late William Robinson, that great gardener, opined that anybody who always went round the garden with secateurs in his pocket was probably a fool, and he was probably to a large extent right. A good rule about pruning is: 'If in doubt, leave the plant alone'. We prune: (1) to encourage growth, flowering and fruitfulness; (2) to keep a tree or a shrub shapely and within bounds if this is necessary; (3) to remove weak or surplus shoots that may be cluttering up the tree or shrub; and of course, (4) to eliminate any dead or diseased shoots or branches.

Always make clean cuts with a sharp knife or secateurs. Any wounds over 1 in (2·5 cm) in diameter should be painted with a wound-sealing compound or a bituminous paint.

Often a tree or a shrub will grow lopsided—a branch, or maybe several, will grow more strongly on one side of the tree than on the other. The temptation is to cut back the strong shoots. This must be firmly resisted and the weaker shoots should be shortened a little to encourage them to grow and balance up the tree.

But pruning is something one learns from a knowledgeable friend if possible—trial and error can be expensive. In my experience, however, trees and shrubs in the flower arranger's garden receive their full pruning treatment and often a good deal more.

Trees, Shrubs & Climbing Plants

Your choice of these must depend to some extent on your soil conditions. There is such a wide and wonderful selection that it seems to me rather like making work for yourself to struggle with things that are unsuited to your conditions. However, gardening is such a challenge anyway that it is sometimes fun to get something growing even when you have been warned against it! All this takes time, so in the first place I would plump for straightforward subjects. Remember to choose for the shape, texture and colour of leaves as well as flowers. Foliage with good winter colour, leaves that reflect the glow of autumn, yellow-greens in early spring to give that feeling of sunlight—all these are important. Winter-flowering shrubs are something I feel everyone should try to grow, especially if you are a flower arranger, as these precious pieces picked in January give more sheer delight than a wealth of bloom in midsummer.

Here then are some trees, shrubs and climbers for colour, leaf sculpture and scent.

Acer   MAPLE

Acer ginnala, height 15–20 ft (4·5–6 m), spread 10 ft (3 m); *A. griseum*, height 15 ft (4·5 m), spread 8–10 ft (2–3 m); *A. negundo* 'Aureum', height 20–25 ft (6–8 m), spread 12–20 ft (4–6 m); *A. pennsylvanicum*, height 18–20 ft (5–6 m), spread 10–12 ft (3–4 m); *A. platanoides*, *A. platanoides* 'Drummondii', height 30–35 ft (9–11 m), spread 12–20 ft (4–6 m); *A. pseudoplatanus* 'Brilliantissimum', *A. pseudoplatanus* 'Nizetii', height 35 ft (11 m), spread 15 ft (4·5 m); *A. rubrum* 'Schlesingeri', height 20–25 ft (6–8 m), spread 8–10 ft (2–3 m).

Maples are worth every inch of space for their lovely coloured foliage, not only in autumn but in spring. Of the large trees, *A. platanoides*, the Norway Maple, is one of the delights of early spring, with the dark branches smothered in lime-green flowers. Its variety 'Drummondii' is a most striking variegated foliage tree, with green leaves that are margined with cream, and are a good colour all summer. *A. pseudoplatanus* 'Nizetii' has foliage ranging in colour from almost white to pale gold, suffused with pink and is excellent for the small garden. *A. rubrum* 'Schlesingeri', the Canadian Red Maple, has wonderful autumn colour. *A. pennsylvanicum* is notable for its beautiful white striated bark and good autumn colour. *A. ginnala* is one of the best for brilliant autumn colour, and has delicate deeply cut leaves. *A. griseum* has bark which peels off to show cinnamon colour beneath, and has particularly good red and scarlet leaves in autumn. *A. negundo* 'Aureum' has bright golden yellow leaves, while *A. pseudoplatanus* 'Brilliantissimum' (one of the best for flower arranging) has young foliage of a soft apricot colour in spring.

Arranging. The flower heads of *A. platanoides* are a joy to arrange in early spring, their brilliant lime green a foil for late daffodils and yellow tulips, or equally lovely in a vase of 'mixed greens'. Next, the new buds and young foliage of *A. pseudoplatanus* 'Brilliantissimum' make this a wonderful tree to pick from, and to look at in the garden, as the leaves usually stay slightly variegated even after the early coral colour has died down to a light green. Stems go beautifully with apricot-coloured tulips, or contrast well with almost-black tulips and white cherry blossom in a black container.

Conditioning and preserving. Conditioning is

most important, for the acers do not last well in water without special care. The stems of *A. platanoides* should be pounded with a hammer and then given a long drink in warm water. The young foliage of *A. pseudoplatanus* 'Brilliantissimum' needs the same treatment, but I find that the early growth of smaller acers lasts better if, after hammering, the leaves are submerged completely under water for a whole night, or longer. The autumn-coloured leaves are always unreliable, though I think it helps a little to submerge the whole stems in a starch solution (made to the strength for table linen on the instructions) instead of just water.

Cultivation. Acers prefer moist soil, in sun or partial shade; *A. rubrum* does best on an acid soil. Plant from October to March. If possible plant acers where they will be protected from cold winds and where the early morning sun will not reach the foliage when it is covered by a spring frost. Acers grown especially for autumn colour need shelter if possible from strong winds, as these will ruin the effect in a day or two. No pruning is usually necessary.

Alnus   ALDER

Alnus incana 'Aurea', height 60–70 ft (18–21 m), spread 20 ft (6 m).

Hardy deciduous trees, water-loving and usually found growing near streams or rivers, alders are beautiful all the year round. As soon as they lose their leaves, the catkins start developing, and with some of the previous year's cones still on the branches, they remain attractive until May or June. *A. incana* 'Aurea' is one of the most attractive, with pink-tinged catkins that appear in January. It is well worth considering if you want a large tree.

Arranging. The branches of fresh young catkins, with small clusters of black cones, provide one of the best outline shapes all through the winter and early spring. A really well-shaped branch can be used for weeks, as the young catkins continue to develop in water. It makes an excellent background for a vase of spring flowers in moss, or for

daffodils, and is a mainstay in many oriental-type arrangements. I often keep the best branches to use in dried groups in the winter.

Conditioning. Hammer the ends of the stems well, and put in warm water for several hours, or overnight if possible.

Cultivation. Plant in any good soil, but not shallow chalky soils; excellent in cold wet places, the alder is exceptionally hardy. Plant October to March. No pruning is usually required.

Aralia

Aralia elata, A. elata 'Aureovariegata', height and spread 20–30 ft (6–9 m).

This is a handsome shrub, it flourishes in the US and does well in the warmth of our town gardens. It has ivy-like flowers and large palmate-type leaves, which in *A. elata* 'Aureo-variegata' are blotched with yellow.

Arranging. I use the well-shaped dark-green leaves of aralia in winter, when I find it a good useful evergreen. The flower heads add interest and are effective in a cream and green group. The larger leaves of *A. elata* 'Aureo-variegata' can only be used on special occasions, when they play a great part at the base of a large summer green arrangement.

Conditioning and preserving. The leaves last better if the stem ends are put into boiling water and then allowed a long drink. It might be worth experimenting with preservation of the green-leaved form in a solution of glycerine and water, though I have not actually done this myself. The seed heads glycerine well in their berried stage.

Cultivation. Plant October to March in any good soil. This aralia is very hardy but gives of its best in warm sheltered gardens. No pruning is normally required.

Arbutus unedo   STRAWBERRY TREE

Height 15–20 ft (4·5–6 m), spread 10–15 ft (3–4·5 m).

Half-hardy evergreen, with white flowers and delightful strawberry-like fruits, which I have enjoyed using in arrangements in America. With a

Arbutus unedo

little care it can be grown successfully in the south of England, and makes a very decorative quick-growing tree.

Arranging. The fruits are the only part of the tree I find useful for arranging. The clusters add interest to any vase, looking particularly well with mixed fruits and red roses, arranged in a dark alabaster vase.

Conditioning. The fruit branches must be well hammered and the leaves must be removed, as the fruits do not last well if the leaves are allowed to take up the moisture. Though the 'strawberries' hang on the stems for a long time, I know of no way to preserve them.

Cultivation. Plant in October for preference, or March to May, in loamy soil. The situation should be sunny and sheltered from cold winds. This species is tolerant of lime. Give protection with straw, bracken or plastic sheeting until the plant is well established. It will then withstand quite strong winds and low temperatures. No pruning is usually needed beyond cutting back straggly shoots in spring to keep the tree shapely.

Aucuba japonica   SPOTTED LAUREL
Height 6–12 ft (2–4 m), spread 5–7 ft (1·5–2 m).

This is a plant I have come to love, despite the fact that for years I felt it only deserved a place in backyard town gardens. It lightens a dull patch,

will grow almost anywhere and is rewarding for picking.

Arranging. A stem of aucuba will help what would otherwise be a monotonous winter green arrangement. I also find that a piece of aucuba or green hellebore can transform a dried group when it starts to look dull after Christmas.

Conditioning. Hammer the ends of the stems and allow a long deep drink. If the arrangement is in a room that is centrally heated, the leaves will stay fresh for much longer if they are given an occasional overhead spray with a little warm water.

Cultivation. Aucubas thrive in any reasonable soil. They may be grown in sun or semi-shade, or in tubs or other containers. Plant in October or March and April. They put up with the atmosphere in town gardens, and of course in the country as well as at the seaside. If grown in a container, feed with a soluble fertilizer according to the maker's instructions throughout the summer. No pruning is normally needed, but if the shrub becomes ungainly, the old stems may be cut hard back to leave only 2–3 ft (60–90 cm). This is best done in April.

Azalea

(Though properly speaking these should appear with *Rhododendron*, I have put them in a separate section for the sake of clarity.)
Deciduous varieties: 'Bouquet de Flore', 'W. S. Churchill', 'Coccinea Speciosa', 'Fire Glow', 'Persil'. Height and spread 5–6 ft (1·5–2 m).
Japanese or evergreen varieties: 'Adonis', 'Blue Danube', 'Orange Beauty', 'Palestrina', 'Vuyk's Scarlet'. Height 2–3 ft (60–90 cm), spread 3–5 ft (1–1·5 m).

These are plants that are well worth the extra effort required to give them the lime-free soil they need. I have had great success with them in one specially prepared area of my garden, and find that it is a corner which gives me more pleasure than almost any other. I value both the flowers in May, giving a wealth of colour, and the lovely tinted autumn foliage. I have limited myself to a choice of one of each colour which I know and like: 'W. S. Churchill', mandarin-red with a brighter red blotch; 'Bouquet de Flore', one of the best salmon-pinks, double; 'Coccinea Speciosa', with semi-double orange-flame coloured flowers, one of my favourites. I think if I were limited, I would grow only the flame colourings ('Fire Glow' is another brilliant one), with 'Persil', white with a pale yellow blotch.

As with roses and dahlias, my advice is always to try to see azaleas in flower before making a choice. I did not do this with my evergreen varieties, and although the foliage is good, I regret having only scarlet and vermilion-flowered plants, when I do not really care for either. I would prefer to plant only white-flowered ones, such as 'Adonis' and 'Palestrina', pure white and creamy white. For those of you who want colour, then I think that 'Vuyk's Scarlet' speaks for itself, as do 'Orange Beauty' and the interesting 'Blue Danube', the nearest thing to a true blue flower. These Japanese azaleas seem to grow well from one side of the United States to the other, from in and around New York to the warmth of California.

Arranging. If you ever have the chance to pick enough, then nothing could be more lovely than a copper pot filled with apricot and pinkish azalea blossom, or a silver wine cooler of the white-flowered varieties with some 'Mount Tacoma' double white tulips. However, I usually feel that only the smallest pieces can be spared from the shrub, to use, for instance, with the early apricot-coloured foliage of *Acer pseudoplatanus* 'Brilliantis-simum' and one or two 'Apricot Beauty' tulips. In October small pieces of the autumn-coloured foliage mix well with dark red or orange dahlias.

Conditioning and preserving. The ends of the stems must be well hammered, and whenever possible allowed an overnight drink in deep water. It is essential to remove all florets as they fade and fall, as they can give the arrangement the appearance of being dead long before it really is. The Japanese varieties take up a glycerine solution well, but I seldom feel one has enough to make this worth while.

Cultivation. Azaleas must have lime-free soil. If the garden soil is alkaline, it is still possible to grow azaleas in specially prepared sites lined with plastic sheeting, or in raised beds (see p. 14). Choose a sheltered site, in full sun, or semi-shade.

Work in peat, hop manure or garden compost at planting time, which may be between October and March. Feed each spring with a general fertilizer as recommended by the makers.

Azaleas appreciate a mulch or layer of half-decayed leaves, peat, or bracken to help conserve moisture and keep the roots cool. They do not like dry conditions. As most azaleas flower early in the spring, they may be damaged by late frosts so they should be planted if possible so that the early morning sun does not fall on the flowers or young shoots while they are still covered with frost.

No pruning is normally required beyond cutting back long or straggly shoots to preserve the shape of the bush. Old, overgrown, misshapen bushes may be cut back hard if necessary and they will usually break into growth again.

Berberis

Berberis 'Buccaneer', height 5–6 ft (1·5–2 m), spread 4–5 ft (1–1·5 m); *B. thunbergii*, *B. thunbergii* 'Atropurpurea' (deciduous), height 4–5 ft (1–1·5m), spread 5–6 ft (1·5–2 m); *B. darwinii*, height and spread 8–10 ft (2·5–3 m); *B. linearifolia* 'Orange King', height 8–10 ft (2–3 m), spread 3–4 ft (around 1 m); *B. verruculosa* (evergreen), height and spread 3–5 ft (1–1.5 m).

Varied shrubs of many different kinds, quite easily grown. The evergreen varieties thrive well in the shade, though I find that for really good autumn colour, the deciduous kinds need full sun. The wide range of heights means that you can find berberis varieties for both the front and back of the border.

B. 'Buccaneer' has lovely coloured berries, pearly pink turning bright red with the red autumn foliage. All the cultivars of *B. thunbergii*, share its pale straw-coloured flowers suffused with red, and superb autumn leaf colour. *B. thunbergii* 'Atropurpurea' has beautiful bronzy-red foliage which is supposed to turn true red in autumn; it does not do this for me, but it is still a lovely shrub, and provides contrast in the border. *B. thunbergii* 'Aurea' has striking golden foliage, turning light green.

The evergreen varieties have good contrast qualities. *B. darwinii* is one of the best, with orange-yellow flowers, purple berries and holly-like leaves. *B. linearifolia* 'Orange King' has the reputation of being one of the most beautiful, deep orange flowers darkening to red in April, and purple berries with greyish bloom. *B. verruculosa* has arching sprays of grey-backed leaves, yellow flowers and purple fruit with a rich bloom.

Arranging. Berberis is one of the great joys to use in arrangements of autumnal coloured fruits and foliage. If you pick small pieces of brilliant colour, you will find that the leaves curl, but the berries will hang on for weeks until they have shrivelled completely. Their arching growth makes them easy to arrange, as they hang grace-fully from any vase, though I think they look their best with autumn groups in copper or brass. I use sprays of *B. verruculosa* for green arrangements in both winter and summer.

Conditioning. Handle with extreme care as the thorns are vicious and can even be poisonous. It is best to remove all thorns for 2–3 in (5–7·5 cm) up the stem; then hammer the ends well and allow a long deep drink in warm water. Though I know of no way to preserve berberis, as I have already mentioned, the berries do stay on their stems for a long time with no special treatment.

Cultivation. Deciduous berberis may be planted from October to March, but the evergreen species are best planted either in September or October, or in March or April. They are not particular about soil; they will even grow quite well on rather poor shallow soils, but they do not like wet or waterlogged ground. Pruning is generally confined to cutting back straggly shoots to keep the bush shapely, or the removal of worn-out old stems. Prune deciduous species in January or February, evergreens after flowering, usually in May or June.

Betula   BIRCH

Betula costata, height 18–20 ft (5–6 m), spread 10–12 ft (3–4 m); *B. papyrifera*, height 20–30 ft (6–9 m), spread 10–15 ft (3–4·5 m); *B. pendula* 'Obelisk', height 15–18 ft 4·5–5 m), spread 3–4 ft (around 1 m); *B. pendula* 'Youngii', height 20–30 ft (6–9 m), spread 10–12 ft (3–4 m).

There is nothing more graceful than a stately silver birch, though I wish so much that I had also grown *B. papyrifera*, which has smooth dazzling white bark, peeling in paper-like layers, and golden leaves in autumn. *B. costata* is another lovely birch, with bark that is a well-marked silver in summer and orange in winter. *B. pendula* 'Youngii' and *B. pendula* 'Obelisk', both weeping forms of our common silver birch, make good subjects for the small garden, delightful in spring with green catkins, with golden colouring in autumn and lovely bark to enjoy all winter.

Arranging. The bursting young catkins and leaves make the branches of silver birch one of the loveliest outlines for a vase of daffodils or moss bed of young spring flowers. The bare branches have such graceful lines that they look beautiful at Christmas painted with clear glue and sprinkled with glitter, used by themselves, with holly berries or with white chrysanthemums.

Conditioning. Like all woody stems, they should be hammered and then allowed a long deep drink.

Cultivation. The birches will grow in any reasonable soil, even hungry shallow soils, but prefer a good rich loam. Plant in sun or shade from October to March; their roots travel a con-siderable distance near the surface, so plant as far away as possible from flower beds.

Buddleia

Buddleia alternifolia, height 12–20 ft (4–6 m), spread 10–15 ft (3–5 m); *B. davidii* 'Black Knight', *B. davidii* 'Harle-quin', height and spread 8–10 ft (2–3 m); *B. fallowiana* 'Alba', height 5–10 ft (1·5–3 m), spread 4–6 ft (1·2–1·8 m).

For a quick effect these are among the best plants and nowadays come in a wonderful colour range, from the common mauve to deepest purple, almost pink or lovely white. The flowers appear at the end of the stems in close spikes of up to 8 in (20 cm). Apart from their rapid growth, a more important reason for including a buddleia in the garden is that they attract butterflies. However, they are not ideal for the flower arrang-er, as they are difficult to keep in water for any length of time.

Arranging. Though effective for a party arrangement, in my experience buddleia is unreliable for more than a day or two. I have used sprays of white buddleia mixed with hoheria, white gladiolus and white chrysanthemums for an August wedding, but I felt it was safe to do this as the flowers only had to last overnight. The deep purple-flowered buddleia looks very good with deep red roses and black grapes.

Conditioning and preserving. As I have mentioned already, I have never found the answer to keeping buddleia for more than two days in water, and I have tried everything. Even for that short time it is advisable to strip off all the foliage, put the stem ends into 1 in (2·5 cm) of boiling water for a minute, and then leave them in deep water for as long as possible.

The seed heads dry well and make a useful contribution as outline for a dried group. They can be picked off the plant when dry, but it is better to pick them before this stage, strip off the leaves and hang them upside down to dry.

Cultivation. Plant from October to March in any reasonably good soil, in sun or semi-shade. Buddleias do not object to a limy soil. *B. fallowiana* is not reliably hardy and should be planted against a south- or west-facing wall. *B. davidii* and its varieties are pruned in February or March. Cut back all the previous year's growth to within about 3 in (7·5 cm) of the point where it left the old stem. Thin out the shoots of *B. alternifolia* in July after flowering; about half to two-thirds of the old stems may be removed. *B. fallowiana* needs little pruning.

Camellia

Camellia japonica 'Mathotiana Alba', 'Elegans', 'Mercury'. *C.* × *williamsii* 'Donation', 'J. C. Williams'. Height and spread 6–12 ft (2–4 m).

The foliage is, for me anyway, almost as beautiful as the flowers. glossy, dark-green rounded leaves on bushes that grow to 6 or 12 ft (2–4 m) high, though in Cornwall and warmer climates they can become huge. They are much hardier than was once thought, though personally I have never had any success in growing them, due I am sure

to bad positioning. They grow well in Washington and many areas of the United States, even where the winters are very severe. Mrs Sydney Thompson in Bethesda, Washington, grew some of the best camellias I have ever seen, so I think I must try again, as they are plants that give me endless pleasure. The whites are my favourites— perhaps because I carried white camellias as my wedding bouquet—especially 'Mathotiana Alba'. Other good ones are 'Elegans', anemone form salmon-rose, 'Mercury', light red, 'Donation' semi-double clear pink, and 'J. C. Williams', pale blush pink.

Arranging. Like me, you may find it difficult to bring yourself to pick these lovely flowers on long stems, though if ever you get the chance, they look well in a silver cake basket and make a spectacular table arrangement. The heads have a habit of falling off, so that it seems wasteful to pick them with long stems, though after the flower is over, I use the remaining stems of foliage and find they last for weeks.

I use camellia foliage after Christmas in mixed green arrangements, for it adds a certain quality that is hard to describe. Years ago we used to put waxed artificial flowers on fresh camellia branches for our contract work in London restaurants, and they not only lasted well but deceived many people, I am sure. Gradually, however, the real buds opened, and were invariably a different colour from the wax flowers, so that really destroyed the illusion.

Conditioning and preserving. There is little I can suggest to prevent the flowers from dropping just as they start to fade, but I think it does help the leaves to last longer if the ends of the stems are burnt and then given a good long drink. Short pieces of foliage take up a glycerine solution well, and are attractive in dried arrangements.

Opposite
The brick path is fringed with wallflowers, *bellis perennis* and other scented spring flowers. On the wall the wistaria and tree peony are about to flower.

Overleaf
Daffodils in the garden in spring with heathers in the background of the picture.

A silver sauceboat makes an ideal container for a handful of colourful spring flowers and blossom. A china sauce-boat would be just as effective.

The bright yellows and golds of daffodils, narcissi and forsythia contrast well in this spring arrangement with the dark tones of an antique wooden mixing bowl. A simple container like this one helps to evoke the impression of wild flowers growing in a woodland setting. The spray of green viburnum foliage in the centre of the arrangement breaks the pattern of the predominating colour and serves as a sharp focal point. The overall effect is one of natural simplicity.

Cultivation. Camellias must have lime-free soil. Plenty of peat or well-decayed leaf-mould should be worked into the ground at planting time. They are best planted in a north- or west-facing position because, as they flower early in the spring, the flowers may be damaged by frost if the early morning sun can reach them. When grown against a wall, see that they do not go short of water or bud dropping may result. Camellias should be planted in September or October, or March and April. *C.* 'J. C. Williams' and *C.* 'Donation' need protection of light woodlands or a west-facing wall. No pruning is normally required, but straggly shoots may be cut back in April.

A beautiful tree that few people plant, yet it is lovely in the spring, and the leaves turn russet gold in the autumn. It grows to the height of a beech or oak, so it needs plenty of space. The green catkins in spring are followed by pretty keys in the autumn which often hang on to the branches long after the leaves have fallen.

Arranging. Spring branches with catkins make a delicate outline for any early arrangement, but I think that the green autumn keys are superb, and I use them as often as possible. They mix well with green zinnias, molucella and lime-green tobacco flowers, and can also make the outline for any foliage arrangement.

Conditioning and preserving. Stems of horn-beam keys should be hammered well and soaked before use. Remove all the leaves to reveal the keys, and they will then last surprisingly well in water.

Carpinus betulus   HORNBEAM
Height around 20 ft (6 m), spread 10–15 ft (3–4·5 m).

If the keys are put into a solution of glycerine and water, they will acquire a slightly glossy appearance and last virtually for ever. They can be dried by hanging the keyed stems upside down after the leaves have been removed, but I am not really happy about this method as they tend to dry too straight. It might be better to leave them in a vase with just a little water, so that they dry off in their natural shapes.

Cultivation. The hornbeam will grow in any good garden soil, in sun or semi-shade. Plant from October to March. No pruning is required.

Cedrus atlantica 'Glauca'   BLUE CEDAR
Height 40–50 ft (12–15 m), spread 15–18 ft (4·5–5 m).

This is a tree for only the largest garden though I did have a friend who loved it so much, and felt that the colour was just what she needed for a certain part of the garden, that she decided to grow one, knowing full well that it would eventually swamp the whole area. I have never been back to find out if she eventually had the courage to cut it down. This wonderful member of the pine family grows into a huge tree, adding an unusual touch of blue-green to the garden, with lovely foliage for flower arranging.

Arranging. Sprays of Blue Cedar are most useful for a winter arrangement, and with some lichen-covered branches and a few grey leaves of *Begonia rex* make a long-lasting winter group. The branches also provide an excellent colour contrast in a vase of 'Christmas greens'.

Conditioning. The ends of the stems should be well hammered and then allowed a long drink of warm water overnight, but try not to leave them in very deep water, as they lose colour when they get very wet: in fact, it is better to remove the lower pine needles so that you have a clear stem below the water level in the vase. If left undisturbed the needles do not drop too badly, and I have managed to keep stems in the house for up to 6 weeks.

Cultivation. Plant in October or November, or in April. Stake the tree firmly and tie one leading shoot to it. It is necessary to keep the leader to one shoot until the tree can no longer be reached as it has a tendency to produce more than one leading shoot. Give a general fertilizer each spring until the tree is growing strongly. Some lower branches may have to be cut away as the tree grows.

Celastrus orbiculatus
Height up to 30 ft (9 m).

This very vigorous deciduous climber is a member of the family that includes the American Bittersweet (*C. scandens*). It is chiefly desirable for its brilliant scarlet seeds, contrasting marvellously with the yellow interiors of the seed capsules. These are not only showy, but also very long-lasting.

Arranging. Sprays of the yellow bracts and red seeds are invaluable for using with autumn-tinted foliage and with dried flower groups.

Preserving. Like the American Bittersweet, berried branches dry well if they are simply hung upside down.

Cultivation. Plant from October to March in any good garden soil. It does not like a very alkaline soil, nor one that lies wet in winter. It is happiest on a south- or west-facing wall, or rambling over an old tree. Where it has plenty of room to spread, no pruning is required, but on walls or pergolas it may have to be kept in bounds by trimming it back in February. Thin out some of the oldest shoots, and cut back long growths to half their length—more severely if necessary.

Chimonanthus praecox   WINTER SWEET
(*C. fragrans*), height and spread 8–10 ft (2·5–3 m).

A hardy deciduous shrub with most sweetly scented winter flowers. They are nondescript, rather like small spiders on a branch, but one small sprig of these pale yellow flowers, deepening to red in the centre, will quickly scent a whole room. My shrub took 7 years to bloom, but it was worth every minute of that long wait.

Arranging. I do not think the flowers show up

Chimonanthus praecox 'Grandiflorus'

well for flower arranging, but they make their presence felt by their fragrance. Tuck a small piece into a spring arrangement, and even if you cannot see it, you will know it is in the vase as soon as you come into the room.

Conditioning. The stems benefit from being put into warm water for a long drink after the ends have been hammered.

Cultivation. This shrub will grow in any soil, but is happiest in a sheltered position against a south- or west-facing wall. Plant from October to March. It may be grown as a free-standing bush in full sun, and will need little or no pruning. Any overcrowding stems may be cut out in March or April. Grown against a wall, the shoots that have flowered need to be pruned back in early spring to leave only about 3 in (7·5 cm) of stem.

Choisya ternata   MEXICAN ORANGE BLOSSOM

Height 5–8 ft (1·5–2·5 m), spread 6–8 ft (around 2 m).

This wonderful shrub with glossy evergreen leaves

produces clusters of white star-like flowers in May, and spasmodically throughout the rest of the year. It forms a rounded bush of aromatic foliage, useful for both the scented flowers and rich green leaves.

Arranging. The foliage is particularly attractive in green arrangements, and can be used to give life to a dried group, especially after Christmas when they tend to look rather dull.

Conditioning and preserving. Hammer the stem ends well, or put them into 1 in (2·5 cm) of boiling water, in either case followed by a long drink before arranging.

Cultivation. Choisyas prefer light well-drained soil and a sheltered position in full sun, although they will tolerate a certain amount of shade. In cold districts they need the protection of a south- or west-facing wall. Even in milder districts young growths may be damaged by frosts. Pruning consists merely of removing straggly shoots, or shortening them by a few inches, and of course cutting back to healthy wood any shoots that have been damaged by frosts. Pruning is best done after flowering in spring, but removal of dead foliage may be done in March or April.

Clematis

Clematis armandii, height 25–30 ft (8–9 m), spread 20–30 ft (6–9 m); *C. macropetala*, height 10–12 ft (3–4 m), spread 6–8 ft (around 2 m); *C. montana, C. montana* 'Rubens', height 30–40 ft (9–12 m), spread 15–20 ft (4·5–6 m); *C. orientalis*, height 15–20 ft (45–6 m), spread 8–10 ft (2–3 m); *C. tangutica*, height and spread 15–20 ft (4·5–6 m). Clematis 'Duchess of Edinburgh', 'Hagley Hybrid', 'Madame le Coultre', 'Nelly Moser', 'W. E. Gladstone', height 8–15 ft (2–4·5 m), spread 4–8 ft (1–2·5 m).

For any wall or fence there is nothing more attractive than a climbing clematis. It is hard to make a choice from the many species and hybrids, so perhaps colour would be your best guide. *C. armandii* is well worth growing for the beautiful evergreen foliage, which provides a good wall cover all winter, and the trusses of ivory white flowers which appear in March and April. *C. macropetala*, has semi-double flowers, pendulous bells of mauve-blue, with lovely seed heads. *C. montana* is a rampant grower with good purple-

Clematis 'Nelly Moser'

stamens; 'Hagley Hybrid', slower in growth but flowering over a long period; 'Nelly Moser', an old favourite and perhaps one of the most widely grown with its mauve-pink flowers, each sepal striped in deep carmine; and 'W. E. Gladstone', with enormous pale lilac blooms that can span 10 in (25 cm).

Arranging. One of the best ways of showing off these beautiful flowers is undoubtedly by floating them in a shallow bowl, and like this they last extremely well and make an attractive table decoration. I love to use one or two clematis as the centre of a group, for they have such a stunning flat face that they show up very distinctly, even from a distance. I have used 'Nelly Moser' like this in many arrangements, mainly because this variety flowers so frequently and well that I feel I can pick them freely. The smaller blooms of *C. montana* 'Rubens' look exquisite arranged alone in a plain or blue glass vase.

Conditioning and preserving. Conditioning is very important, as the flowers do not normally last well, though I do remember at a dinner given for the late Constance Spry in Sydney, Australia, the table was arranged with clematis, and when they started to fade two of us put a few in our glasses where a little champagne was left, and the blooms revived in seconds. So you could try using champagne if you think it worth it! Presumably this is the basis of the Japanese treatment for wisteria and clematis—they dip the ends of the stems in pure alcohol for a few hours. I put the ends of the stems into a little boiling water for a few moments, taking extra care that the steam does not reach the delicate flowers, and then if possible leave them overnight in water before arranging. I find they last very well in Oasis if given a long drink beforehand, but there seems to be no way of guaranteeing that the flowers will not drop very quickly in spite of all your effort. One good thing is that they can be replaced very easily if they do die.

Only the seed heads can be preserved successfully, and these are of great value for small arrangements in winter. Leave them to dry on the plant, and then spray the fluffy heads with light hair lacquer before they are blown away.

tinged foliage and a wealth of single open white flowers (or pink in the case of *C. montana* 'Rubens'). *C. orientalis* 'Orange Peel' has delightful nodding heads of four thick petals resembling orange peel, which flower in September and October. *C. tangutica* flowers in August, and the pointed pendent little yellow lanterns are followed by good seed heads. Among the large-flowered hybrids, I would recommend 'Duchess of Edinburgh', with fragrant double white rosette-shaped flowers; 'Madame le Coultre', which has large blooms of single white flowers with yellow

Cultivation. Clematis prefer an alkaline soil, but will grow reasonably well in any reasonable garden soil. They like to be in full sun, but they also like to have their roots in the shade, so it is wise to plant some dwarf shrubs at their base. When grown against a wall, they may need watering in dry spells. Plant from October to May. Pruning requirements vary with the different species and hybrids. Thin out shoots of *C. armandii* in February; *C. macropetala* and *C. montana* may be thinned out after flowering and new shoots trained in. Prune *C. orientalis* in spring if necessary, thinning out old shoots and shortening new ones if necessary; prune *C. tangutica* in March, cutting previous year's shoots to within 2–3 in (5–7 cm) of the base. The newly planted specimens of the foregoing may be cut back by about one-third of their length immediately after planting. The other clematis described, the hybrids, may be pruned hard back in February. Cut all shoots made in the previous year just above a joint, at about 12 in (30 cm) from the base. It is important to cut plants back to 6–9 in (15–23 cm) immediately after planting.

Cornus DOGWOOD

Cornus alba, C. alba 'Sibirica', *C. alba* 'Spaethii', height 8–10 ft (2–3 m), spread 6–10 ft (2–3 m); *C. florida*, height 10–12 ft (3–4 m), spread 20–25 ft (6–8 m); *C. kousa*, height and spread 8–10 ft (2·5–3m); *C. mas*, height 8–12 ft (2·5–4 m), spread 8–10 ft (2·5–3 m); *C. nuttallii*, height 15–20 ft (4·5–6 m), spread 8–12 ft (2·5–4 m). All deciduous shrubs.

C. alba is a spreading Siberian shrub with brilliant red shoots in winter; *C. alba* 'Sibirica Variegata' has the added attraction of silver variegated foliage, and *C. alba* 'Spaethii' has golden variegated leaves. *C. sanguinea*, with red and black berries, grows wild and was used for making arrows in bygone days as the wood is extremely hard. But of all the cornus, *C. florida*, the American dogwood, is one of the most beautiful sights in the world. It is the state flower of Virginia, and is found growing wild in many areas there, the small yellowish flowers of *C. florida*, and the rosy-red bracts of the pink form, *C. florida* 'Rubra', producing sheets of pink during May in many places in the eastern areas of the United States. *C. nuttallii*, the Pacific dogwood, with buttons of white flowers surrounded by six creamy-white petal-like bracts. Frances Perry says that the bark of this tree made quinine substitute, and was greatly treasured in the American Civil War when real quinine was unobtainable because of the blockades. *C. kousa*, a tall, elegant Japanese shrub with white bracts growing along slender branches, may be one of the best varieties for Great Britain. *C. mas*, is one that I have grown, and it is a sheer delight, with a mass of small clustered yellow flowers in February, well worth growing on account of its early flowers alone. It is a native of southern Europe, and its very hard wood is reputed to have been that used for making the Trojan wooden horse.

Arranging. I use the tall red shoots of *C. alba* in green winter groups; although they lose some of their brilliant colour in the house, they are still distinctly red, and the shape of the bare stems as well as their colour will enhance any arrangement. If I can ever get any of the American dogwood, I love to use it in any form. When in flower it is superb in a vase by itself, as also are a few branches in autumn when the leaves have turned to a russet-red colour. The delicate bare branches of silver bark are a delight in winter, especially when used to make the outline for an oriental type of arrangement.

I pick small pieces of *C. mas* in January and force them out in a warm room; they open well and give a touch of colour to a few early spring bulbs.

Conditioning and preserving. The stems should be pounded with a hammer, and then given at least twelve hours in water. This applies whether you are using flowering stems or branches of foliage.

I have seen a vase of preserved American dogwood that had been put into a flower-drying powder by Mrs Prewitt of Lexington, and I have never seen anything so beautiful in my life. I had to go and touch the flowers, and even then, on that chill November day, found it hard to believe my eyes.

Cultivation. Plant from October to March. They will succeed in partial shade, but the full colour of the stems is developed in a sunny situation. Any good garden soil is suitable, and they enjoy a moist situation. No pruning is usually necessary except that the species and varieties such as *C. alba*, which are grown for their highly coloured stems in winter, should be cut hard back almost to ground level in April.

Corylopsis

Corylopsis pauciflora, height 4–5 ft (1–1·5 m), spread 6–10 ft (2–3 m); *C. spicata*, height and spread 4–6 ft (1–2 m).

These delightful deciduous shrubs are not widely enough grown, to my way of thinking. *C. pauciflora* is a densely branched shrub with small hanging yellow catkin-like flowers, sweetly scented and flowering in early spring. *C. spicata* grows a little taller and has similar flowers, but with rounded, more glaucous leaves.

Arranging. A few stems of corylopsis with delicate little pale catkins look exceptionally pretty with a few daffodils or early species of tulips.

Corylopsis pauciflora

Conditioning. Hammer the ends of the stems well before giving them a long drink of water.

Cultivation. Plant October to March, if possible in lime-free soil, in sun or partial shade or, preferably, in thin woodland or against a south- or west-facing wall. As these shrubs flower early in the spring there is the danger of the blooms being damaged if early morning sun can reach them when they are covered with frost. If the soil is alkaline, work in plenty of moist peat—a 2 gallon (9 l) bucketful, to the square yard (sq m) at planting time. No pruning beyond the removal of old or weak shoots is usually necessary with this plant.

Corylus — HAZEL

Corylus avellana 'Contorta', height and spread 8–10 ft (2·5–3 m); *C. maxima* 'Purpurea', height and spread 18–20 ft (5–6 m).

The deciduous hazel family is lovely in the wild form, with dancing yellow catkins on an early spring day. *C. avellana* 'Contorta', the Corkscrew Hazel, or Crazy Filbert as it is called in Australia, has great charm in winter and early spring, with attractively twisted branches and small catkin flowers. *C. maxima* 'Purpurea' has wonderful coloured foliage which rivals the copper beech for colour, and its catkins are a gorgeous pinky red.

Arranging. The contorted hazel is a 'must' for the flower arranger's garden: I use it continually, as a background for a line arrangement, or as outline for a green group. The catkins of the purple hazel are a delight, and so is the purple foliage—but it should not be cut until the leaves have matured on the branch a little, as it will then last very much longer in water.

Conditioning. Hammer the woody stems well before giving a long drink.

Cultivation. Plant in any good garden soil from October to March, in sun or partial shade—preferably in sun, but where they are protected from bitter north and east winds. Avoid wet or waterlogged sites. For the first few years encourage the plants to become bushy by cutting the new shoots back in spring by half their

Corylus avellana 'Contorta'

length. Then shorten shoots a little after flowering in March or April to maintain the production of flowering side shoots. If the bush becomes congested in later years, thin out some of the old stems in late summer or autumn.

Cotinus (RHUS)

Cotinus coggygria 'Flame', 'Foliis Purpureis', height and spread 8–10 ft (2·5–3 m).

These deciduous smoke-bush trees are mainly grown for their coloured autumn foliage, but the common name comes from the smoke-like flower plumes which often remain on the bush until autumn. 'Flame' is reputed by Hillier to have brilliant orange-red foliage in autumn, whereas 'Foliis Purpureis' has, as its name implies, ruby red foliage and plumes of red flowers. If you are going to buy only one bush, it is always difficult to choose which to have, but I think my preference would be for the 'Foliis Purpureis' as it is more effective for a longer period. Sadly I lost mine quite suddenly, but have no idea why.

Arranging. The leaves will not last well in water until they are mature. Then pieces of the red foliage look wonderful with the mixed reds of roses, gladioli, dahlias and autumn-coloured foliages and berries. The green-leaved varieties have more effective flower heads for the arranger.

Conditioning. Put the ends of the stems into 1 in (2·5 cm) of boiling water, and then submerge the whole branch overnight. No foliage should be picked until it has been in full leaf for several weeks, unless you are prepared to change it as it droops.

Cultivation. Plant from October to March in any reasonably fertile, well-drained garden soil, in full sun. Do not feed these shrubs if their glorious autumn colours are desired. Any pruning to keep the tree shapely is best done in March or April each year.

Cotoneaster

Cotoneaster 'Cornubia', height and spread 15–20 ft (4·5–6 m); *C. horizontalis*, height 2 ft (60 cm), spread 6–7 ft (around 2 m); *C. wardii*, height 5–8 ft (1·5–2·5 m), spread 3–7 ft (1–2 m); *C. watereri*, height and spread 10–15 ft (3–4·5 m).

A large collection of ornamental evergreen or semi-evergreen shrubs, varying from prostrate forms to small trees. The majority are deciduous and all have good autumn colour. *C.* 'Cornubia', which grows into a small tree, has in addition to lovely autumnal colour, large clusters of red berries which often remain on their branches until after Christmas. The flat-growing *C. horizontalis*, the 'herringbone cotoneaster', grows well against a wall or fence or flat on the ground and has the rather curious tendency of attracting queen wasps —I have managed to kill many in the spring. *C. wardii* is a stiff, erect, medium-sized shrub with evergreen leaves, glossy on the top and white underneath, and sprays of bright orange-red berries. *C. watereri*, is a fast-growing shrub, in form a little like *C.* 'Cornubia', with a wealth of berries which I find that the birds scatter, so that I now have several seedlings.

Arranging. Though I am sometimes tempted to pick one or two arching sprays of the delicate white flowers, I do so reluctantly, for it is the later sprays of berries that are my chief delight. They last so well that I find I can often keep them in a vase for several weeks. I use small pieces from November onwards, when they start to colour, and I find them a great help at Christmas if the holly is not berrying well. They are handsome used with mixed foliage groups, or with apricot-coloured dahlias, gladioli, late roses and other autumn flowers.

Conditioning. Hammer the ends of the stems well before putting into deep water overnight.

Cultivation. Cotoneasters will grow in any soil, even the poorest. They like a sunny position, but will tolerate some shade. Plant from October to March. Little pruning is needed, but if the plants are growing too strongly they may be cut back in spring to keep them within bounds.

Daphne

Daphne cneorum (Garland Flower), height 6 in (15 cm), spread 2–3 ft (60–90 cm); *D. laureola*, height 2–4 ft (60 cm–1·2 m), spread 3–6 ft (1–2 m); *D. mezereum*, *D. mezereum* 'Alba', height 3–5 ft (1–1·5 m), spread 2–4 ft (60 cm–1·2 m); *D. odora* 'Aureomarginata', height 3–5 ft (1–1·5 m), spread 4–6 ft (1–2 m).

A family of moderate-sized shrubs, suitable for a small garden or even a rock garden, and sweetly scented. *D. cneorum*, evergreen is best for the rock garden, with clusters of very fragrant deep pink flowers on prostrate branches in May. *D. laureola* is an evergreen and useful for a shady corner, as well as being good for arranging in winter. *D. mezereum*, with rose-mauve flowers, and *D. mezereum* 'Alba', deciduous, with white flowers, are so fragrant and often flower as early as January, a mass of colour before the leaves appear. The only snag is that this is a short-lived shrub, though easy to grow from seed. *D. odora* 'Aureomarginata' has gorgeous lemony-scented flowers: I always wore a small piece as soon as it arrived in the shop from Cornwall in January.

Arranging. Both *D. mezereum* and *D. odora* make their presence felt as soon as they are brought into the house, whatever you do with them. A piece of *D. mezereum* will add height, colour and fragrance to a moss garden. *D. odora* is pretty just on its own in any decorative small vase or piece of china.

Conditioning. Put the ends of the stems into boiling water for one minute, and then let them have a long drink.

Cultivation. Daphnes are best planted in September or October, or in March or April. They thrive in any good garden soil and do not object to chalky soil. Plant in sun or partial shade, but make sure the site is well drained. No pruning is normally required beyond keeping the plants shapely by trimming back unwanted growths in March.

Opposite
1 *Cornus mas*
2 Iris
3 Daffodil
4 Leucojum *summer snowdrop*
5 Hellebore
6 Primrose
7 Tellima
8 Petasites
9 Bergenia
10 Hellebore
11 *Scilla tubergeniana*

Small bunches of spring flowers are tucked into a bed of moss and arranged on a plate in a trivet-stand. To prevent the water from being siphoned off, the moss is set on some wire netting so that it does not touch the water.

Elaeagnus

Elaeagnus pungens 'Maculata', *E. pungens* 'Variegata', height and spread up to 10 ft (3 m).

The only members of this family that I would grow are *E. pungens* 'Maculata', a shrub with thick leathery leaves in two shades of superb green, heavily splashed with yellow-gold in winter; and *E. pungens* 'Variegata', with cream-yellow marginal variegation. Both plants bring a touch of sunlight in winter, and I cannot recommend these evergreens too highly.

Arranging. The vivid colouring of these leaves provides excellent contrast in mixed green arrangements, and also makes good background material for the first daffodils.

Conditioning and preserving. All varieties last well in water. The ends of the stems should be put in boiling water, or hammered well, and then given a long deep drink.

Elaeagnus takes up a glycerine solution very well. Hammer the stem ends well, and leave them standing in the solution in strong light for best results, for about 4 weeks, or until you can see the change in colour.

Cultivation. Plant in September or October, or in April in any soil, even thin sandy or limy soils, in full sun or in partial shade. No pruning beyond trimming straggly shoots in April is normally required. Sometimes the variegated form produces green shoots which should be cut out at the base.

Erica and Calluna

Erica carnea, height 6–12 in (15–30 cm), spread 18–24 in (45–60 cm); *E. mediterranea*, height 6–10 ft (2–3 m), spread 3–4 ft (around 1 m); *Calluna vulgaris* 'H. E. Beale', height 9 in (23 cm), spread 2 ft (60 cm).

Small heathers with flowers ranging in colour from white through pinks to reds, the ericas make good ground cover, and it is possible to choose your varieties so that you have some in flower every month of the year. Several varieties have the added attraction of golden or russet foliage in the autumn.

E. carnea 'Springwood Pink' and 'Springwood White' flower from December to March; 'Eileen Porter' has deep carmine red flowers from October to April. *E. mediterranea* 'Superba' with pink flowers from March to May, and 'W. T. Rackliff' perhaps the best white, flowering from March to April, and a little taller. Best of all for the flower arranger is the Ling, *Calluna vulgaris* 'H. E. Beale', with long spikes of deep pink double flowers in September and October.

Arranging. I think in all fairness it must be said that heathers are not particularly good for flower arranging, but are worth growing for continuous colour in the garden. Nevertheless, I do like to use some small pieces in a spring vase, for even though they do not last well and shed their foliage, they do not look really dead.

Conditioning and preserving. There is little I can suggest to make these flowers last well in water. The flower spikes of 'H. E. Beale' once arranged will dry off in water, only needing an occasional dusting! I have also been recommended to try sticking the stems into a potato, the moisture from which will keep the heather fresh and the colour good as it gradually dries off.

Cultivation. Plant in October or November, March, April or May. *E. carnea* and its varieties grow on any soil, acid or alkaline, and *E. mediterranea* does not mind some lime in the soil. *Calluna vulgaris*, however, does not like lime, and plenty of peat should be worked into the soil for this species and its varieties. Plant in full sun. See that the plants never go short of water, especially in the first year or two after planting.

Eucalyptus

Eucalyptus gunnii, height 40 ft (12 m), spread 15 ft (4·5 m); *E. parviflora*, height and spread 30 ft (9 m).

Gum Trees are natives of Australia and Tasmania and most are not very hardy here, so I have included only two species, both of which I feel are fairly reliable in milder parts. If you live in California, Florida or Australia, then of course your choice is unlimited. The eucalyptus makes a tall, elegant tree that sheds its bark but not its leaves. *E. gunnii* has rounded leaves and very grey young foliage, but *E. parviflora* is hardier here.

Arranging. The grey-silver leaves of eucalyptus last well in water, and there is nothing better for a winter vase, with stems of grey lichen-covered branches, and some leaves of *Begonia rex*. It can be used in large groups in January, when it comes into the flower markets from southern France.

Conditioning and preserving. The ends of the stems should be hammered or put into boiling water, before being given a long drink.

Eucalyptus stems take up a glycerine solution very well and turn a lovely grey-brown colour, and make a wonderful background for lighter dried seed heads and grasses. Hammer the stems well and leave them in the solution for several weeks. Some people add a little brown dye to the mixture, and this strengthens the leaf colour. They are very expensive to buy in dried form, but I think they are probably worth it, since they last for weeks, or even years.

Cultivation. Eucalyptus like a well-drained, good garden soil and a sunny situation. Plant in June or July. See that they do not go short of water in the first two or three years after planting. No pruning is normally needed, but to provide plenty of foliage for cutting the trees may be 'stooled'— that is, the shoots are cut back to the base every year. Eucalyptus need to be given the support of strong stakes for the first three or four years after planting.

Euonymus

Euonymus europaeus, height 6–10 ft (2–3 m), spread 5–10 ft (1·5–3 m); *E. fortunei* 'Silver Queen', height 6–10 ft (2–3 m), spread 4·–6 ft (1–2 m); *E. japonicus* 'Aureo-pictus', 'Microphyllus Variegatus', 'Ovatus Aureus', height 10–15 ft (3–4·5 m), spread 5–8 ft (1·5–2·5 m).

A family of widely different shrubs, both evergreen and deciduous, though I think the slow-growing waxy-leaved evergreens are particularly useful for flower arrangers, as they are at their best in winter and early spring and many have silver or yellow variegated leaves.

E. europaeus, the spindle tree and a native of southern England, is a deciduous tree with fine coloured leaves in autumn and attractive pink capsules enclosing bright orange seeds. Among the best evergreens are: *E. fortunei* 'Silver Queen', with good green and white variegated leaves, a small spreading shrub that can also be induced to cover walls; *E. japonicus* 'Aureo-pictus', with shiny green and gold leaves that revert easily, but are still excellent for the flower arranger as they last so well in water; *E. japonicus* 'Microphyllus Variegatus', its very small leaves with a silver margin; and *E. japonicus* 'Ovatus Aureus' with leaves suffused and blotched yellow.

Arranging. Branches of the spindle tree, in the ornamental berrying stage, are an excellent foil to dried groups, and also go well with autumn arrangements in shades of pink and apricot. The variegated evergreen leaves add graceful lines and light touches to winter flower arrangements and mixed greens.

Conditioning. Hammer the stem ends well before soaking in warm water for several hours.

Cultivation. Euonymus will thrive in sun or partial shade in any good garden soil. Plant in September or October, March or April. Give the variegated forms some shelter—a wall, or other shrubs, against cold winds if possible. No pruning except to keep the shrubs shapely is usually needed, and any that has to be done may be done in February or March.

Fagus sylvatica   BEECH

Fagus sylvatica purpurea 'Atropunicea', *F. sylvatica* 'Heterophylla Laciniata', *F. sylvatica* 'Tricolor', height 15–18 ft (4·5–5·5 m), spread 12–15 ft (4–4·5 m).

Far too large for the average garden, do consider planting one of these huge deciduous trees for your children's children if you have the space and a suitably chalky soil. *F. sylvatica purpurea* 'Atropunicea' is a fine form with extra-dark purple leaves. *F. sylvatica* 'Heterophylla Laciniata' is one of the fern-leaved beeches and a very lovely tree. *F. sylvatica* 'Tricolor' is a really beautiful tree, popular in the United States but not widely grown here, though it deserves to be with its swinging cream, pink and maroon leaves.

Arranging. A stem of beech makes a fine background to any vase, especially in the autumn. I love to use copper beech with regale lilies, or as a background for dahlias, autumn berries and foliages.

Conditioning and preserving. The mature stems should have their ends hammered and then left in deep water overnight. Young beech branches benefit from being totally submerged overnight, after the usual hammering treatment, of course.

To preserve beech, stand the stem ends in a solution of glycerine and water and leave until the foliage turns colour. It is best to use leaves that are not too old for this—in about July or August. Autumn-coloured leaves can be preserved by pressing the sprays under a carpet for several days.

Cultivation. The beeches thrive on all soils, alkaline or acid, provided they are not waterlogged, and they enjoy full sun. Plant from October to March. No pruning is required.

Forsythia

F. × intermedia 'Lynwood', 'Primulina', 'Spectabilis', *F. suspensa* 'Fortunei', height and spread 8 or 9 ft (around 2·6 m).

One of the joys of early spring, with golden-yellow bell-shaped flowers that wreath the brown branches, on deciduous shrubs that grow up to 8 or 9 ft (around 2·6 m). Forsythias are easy to grow and most rewarding, especially as they seem to flourish on hard pruning—or maybe, in my case, hard picking. 'Lynwood' has the largest golden flowers, borne in profusion along the branches; 'Primulina' is one of my favourites as the flowers are an exquisite primrose yellow: 'Spectabilis' is still deservedly one of the most popular; and *F. suspensa* 'Fortunei' has arching branches and leaves of good autumn colour.

Arranging. This is a good subject for forcing, so stems can be taken into the house in early January to produce flowering branches about five weeks later. I use them at any length, depending on the arrangement: small pieces for a moss garden to give the essential height, or large sprays for mixing with daffodils. It is one shrub that will tolerate near-slaughter, so one need have no scruples about cutting it hard. I also use the autumn-tinted foliage.

Conditioning. To force, hammer the stems well, place in warm water, and keep in a warm room. Change the water daily and remember to keep it warm.

Cultivation. Plant forsythias from October to March or April. They thrive in full sun, but tolerate partial shade and will grow in any normal garden soil in town or country or at the seaside. They should be pruned after flowering by shortening shoots that have borne flowers by about a third of their length. Remove completely any old and worn-out shoots.

Garrya elliptica

Height 8–15 ft (2·5–4·5 m), spread 6–12 ft (2–4 m).

I first grew this evergreen shrub because I was told that it would flourish even on a north wall,

Garrya elliptica

though in fact I now know it needs some protection in colder districts during winter. I feel it is a 'must' for both the gardener and the flower arranger, with beautiful grey catkins, particularly long on the male plants, and attractively clustered grey-green foliage. It can make a beautiful specimen tree if pruned well and allowed an island site, but in colder areas does well as a wall shrub. Mine grew so rapidly that my husband always said he didn't know why I wanted more windows in our cottage when I covered them all with garrya.

Arrangement. This is a shrub that I cannot praise too highly. I use the catkins from December to February, on any length of stem from large branches of 4 ft (1·2 m) to smaller pieces. It looks particularly fine in all green arrangements with *Aucuba japonica*, or with lichen-covered branches and bergenia leaves, or as a background for Christmas arrangements.

Conditioning and preserving. The stems should be pounded with a hammer and then allowed a long drink of water. At the Chelsea show one year I noticed on the NFAS stand that they had glycerined stems of garrya, so I have since tried

this too, and find it results in dark brown stems with attractive catkins still firm on their branches.

Cultivation. Thriving in sun or shade *G. elliptica* should be planted in April with as little root disturbance as possible—buy container-grown plants. Any well-drained reasonable garden soil is suitable, and against a west- or south-facing wall is the best site for this shrub. Whenever possible plant in a sunny spot, although some partial shade is tolerated. No pruning is necessary beyond keeping the shrub in bounds.

Hamamelis WITCH HAZEL

Hamamelis mollis, H. mollis 'Pallida', height and spread 8–12 ft (2·5–4 m); *H. virginiana*, height and spread 8–12 ft (2·5–4 m).

H. mollis is one of the most attractive deciduous shrubs to grow and to arrange, with small yellow fragrant flowers rather like spiders blooming on bare branches from December to March, and good yellowish autumn foliage. 'Pallida', with dense primrose-coloured flowers, is a form I would love to grow too. The shrub from which we extract witch hazel lotion is *H. virginiana*, a native of America, where I have seen it growing on the Blue Mountains of Virginia. Unlike *H. mollis*, the flowers appear after the leaves, in September, but the shrub is well worth growing for its brilliant autumn leaf colour.

Arranging. Winter-flowering shrubs are of course the most valuable of all material for the flower arranger, and pieces of *H. mollis* will enhance any early spring arrangement. It can be used on short stems or long, depending on what you can spare from your plant.

Conditioning. Hammer the stem ends well and then give a long drink of water.

Cultivation. Plant from October to March in any well-drained ordinary garden soil provided it is not limy. *H. mollis* and its varieties enjoy full sun or partial shade, and shelter from bitter north or east winds. Give *H. virginiana* a more shaded, sheltered situation. No pruning other than cutting back straggly branches after flowering to keep the tree shapely is needed.

Hedera colchica 'Dentata Variegata'

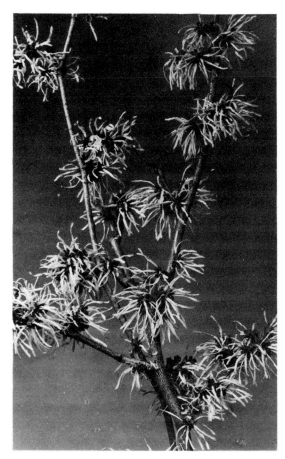

Hamamelis mollis 'Pallida'

Hedera   IVY

Hedera canariensis 'Variegata', height and spread 20 ft
(6 m); *H. colchica* 'Dentata Variegata', height and spread
20–30 ft (6–9 m); *H. helix* 'Buttercup', height and spread
6 ft (2 m); *H. helix* 'Gold Heart', height and spread 8 ft
(2·5 m).

Climbing evergreen plants that have retrieved
some of their former popularity these last few
years. It is interesting that most catalogues now
say a well-built wall will not suffer if ivies are
grown on it. I hope this is true, or my cottage
could fall down round my ears at any moment!
Self-clinging, with heart-shaped leaves, they make
a wonderful contribution to a garden, and those
with good variegation are also excellent for picking. *H. canariensis* 'Variegata' has shield-shaped
olive green leaves with silver and white edging,
pink tinted when young. *H. colchica* 'Dentata
Variegata' has large leaves of soft green, with deep
yellow variegation. *H. helix* 'Buttercup' has small
bright gold leaves, while 'Gold Heart' (or
'Jubilee') is a fast-growing ivy of great distinction,
the leaves dark green with a gold centre.

Arranging. Ivies are wonderful for using in
midwinter, arranged on their own in a wall vase,
or placed somewhere where they can fall naturally.
Sprays can be used in a green arrangement to
provide the falling line that softens the whole
effect.

45

Conditioning and preserving. Put the ends of the stems into boiling water for a few moments, then leave in cold water overnight, and you will find that the sprays last marvellously well.

Stems of ivy and berries take up a solution of glycerine and water very well. They should be left in the solution for several weeks, when they will change colour from green to greeny-brown, and in that state will last for months.

Cultivation. One useful tip: when taking a cutting, lay it along the ground and not, as so many people try to do, up the wall. Plant from September to March in any good garden soil and in any situation, sunny or in partial shade. The variegated ivies develop their best colour in full sun. No pruning is necessary, but the old leaves should be clipped over every spring, and of course the plants must be cut back whenever they are escaping beyond their allotted space—especially if they are beginning to penetrate under tiles or slates.

Hydrangea

Hydrangea arborescens, height and spread 4–6 ft (1–2 m); *H. macrophylla hortensis*, height and spread 4–6 ft (1–2 m); *H. paniculata*, height and spread 10–15 ft (3–4·5 m); *H. quercifolia*, height and spread 4–6 ft (1–2 m); *H. sargentiana*, height and spread 8–10 ft (2·5–3 m).

The wonderful range of shades of pink, blue and white makes these plants most valuable for the garden and for cutting. They bloom for several months, and have the added attraction of drying well with heads that keep their colour and are so useful all winter. *H. hortensis* is the most commonly grown and gives wonderful colour effects. *H. arborescens* is one of my favourites as the flowers are more delicate in form, having rounded heads on slender stems. The creamy-white colour soon fades to lime green, making it particularly useful in all stages of the flowering period. *H. paniculata* is heavenly if it grows well for you; I have tried to grow it endless times but it is not at all happy in my garden. It seems to enjoy the northern climes and grows well in the North of Scotland and in North America. Both *H. arborescens* and *H. paniculata* flower on the new wood,

so they need fairly hard, careful pruning each year. *H. sargentiana*, which grows tall and looks very decorative in the garden, is, I find, quite difficult to arrange. *H. quercifolia*, sometimes known as the Oak Leaf hydrangea, has superb autumnal tints in the foliage and lasts surprisingly well when cut. Again, it is a flower I have used most successfully in America.

Arranging. Hydrangea heads need to be well matured on the plant before you cut them for an arrangement, having been out on the bush for over a week. The heads will then stand well and provide solid colour value in the centre of the vase. Use them in a massed arrangement with all the hydrangea colours mixed. You can also use the white heads for a green and white arrangement, the blues with blue and mauve, or with the spiky heads of pink and purple larkspur and delphiniums, pink roses, etc. As the heads turn green they will then contribute much to a foliage and green arrangement, the heads of *H. arborescens* being particularly attractive.

Conditioning and preserving. All heads last better if the ends of the stems are placed in 1 in (2·5 cm) of boiling water and then given a long drink up to their necks in water. Spraying the heads with one of the small mist sprays you can buy now is invaluable, and if the blooms are very young I find that keeping them in water overnight with the heads covered in wet paper helps them to stay much fresher. For the best results in preserving the flower heads for winter I find that they dry well with the ends of the stems in water and the heads in a warm, dry atmosphere—the kitchen or the linen cupboard, for example. The heads keep their colour much better if they are dried quickly. For a satiny brown head you can stand the stems of the flower heads in a solution of glycerine and water. They turn brown and make a most unusual arrangement.

Cultivation. Plant from October to April in good garden soil which has had peat, manure or compost worked into it. They will thrive in full sun or light shade, and should be so sited that the early morning sun does not reach the tender new shoots on a frosty morning. Mulch annually with suitable material in April. Leave flower heads on the stems until March. Cut out weak shoots in March if the bush is congested, and on old plants of *H. macrophylla* cut out some shoots at ground level every year to encourage new growth.

Jasminum   JASMINE

Jasminum nudiflorum, height and spread 9–10 ft (around 3 m); *J. officinale* 'Affine', height up to 30 ft (9 m), spread 6–10 ft (2–3 m).

Jasmine is one of the most popular climbers and is simple to grow. The little yellow flowers of *J. nudiflorum*, winter jasmine, cheer any winter day, grow easily and cover a wall quite quickly.

J. officinale is the sweetly scented summer white jasmine, of which 'Affine' is the best form. Nothing gives more pleasure than the perfume of these blooms on a summer night, so I grow the plant under my windows.

Arranging. Little stalks of winter jasmine go beautifully with the first snowdrops and crocus, and can be used to give height to a moss garden. Arranged with variegated holly and Christmas roses, it makes a perfect Christmas arrangement. Pieces of white summer jasmine will scent any room and do not need to be specially arranged.

Conditioning and preserving. Both types benefit from having the stem ends dipped in boiling water and left in cool water for an hour.

The winter jasmine can be preserved in any flower drying powder.

Cultivation. Plant from September to April in any good garden soil. These two species like full sun but will be quite happy if planted on an east or north-facing wall. They need some support—*J. nudiflorum* loves to be trained round a 6 ft (2 m) high wigwam of bean poles or against a wall or fence. So does *J. officinale*, but, left to ramble up through a tree, it will reach 30 ft (9 m).

Lavandula   LAVENDER

Lavandula spica, L. spica 'Hidcote', *L. vera*, height around 3 ft (90 cm).

Lavenders are valued for their fragrance, and for their long period of flowering. The tallest grow to about 3 ft (90 cm), are good for hedging in a small garden, and make an attractive edging round a large rose bed. *L. spica* 'Hidcote' is my favourite for compact growth, a wealth of deepest purple-blue flowers and grey foliage. There are now several improved forms of *L. spica* (old English lavender) with good grey foliage and long spikes of pale mauve flowers. *L. vera* (Dutch lavender), with broader silver leaves and tall soft-mauve flowers, is the one from which the oil is extracted.

Arranging. These mauve spikes add outline and a touch of colour to a small vase of 'pinks' in mid-summer, and are nice too for their fragrance.

Conditioning and preserving. The flower spikes seem to last well with no special treatment. They even dry off in the vase of water.

To preserve for winter use for sachets, or so that you can have spikes to use in winter arrangements, cut the stems when the flowers are fully open, usually at the end of July, bunch together and hang upside down in a warm place to dry quickly. I well remember seeing bunches hung up in the linen cupboard at home when I was a child.

Cultivation. Plant from October to April in any good garden soil, in full sun. Lavenders will grow in semi-shade but tend to be soft and lanky. Pruning consists of trimming the new growths back in August or September. It is not wise to cut into old wood—far better to trim the young growths to keep the plants shapely.

Ligustrum   PRIVET

Ligustrum lucidum 'Golden Wax', height and spread 6 ft (2 m); *L. ovalifolium* 'Aureum'; *L. vulgare*, height 5 ft (1·5 m), spread 3 ft (1 m).

One of the most useful evergreen shrubs in its own right, rather than for hedging as most of us think of it. I use golden privet all the year round, and find that it is a wonderful standby. I mention the common privet, *L. vulgare*, not because it is an ideal garden plant, unless you have lots of room, but because I do like to pick the delicate berried sprays in autumn. The smaller-leafed variety which is widely grown in America is also very effective, but as much disregarded there as ours is here—

though for flower arrangement it really is *so* useful. I have just ordered the cultivar *L.* 'Golden Wax', with waxy yellow leaves, and hope it will prove as invaluable.

Arranging. This is one plant that I find these days I can hardly live without. I use stems from 4 in (10 cm) long up to 4 ft (1·2 m) for large church groups, and find that it makes a good background for almost any flower arrangement. The delicate leaf form and light foliage of the golden privets are ideal. My sister has a large clump of golden privet, and is in favour with the cathedral flower arrangers, as they use it all the year round; and she is lucky too, since this constant heavy pruning is just what is needed to keep the golden colour.

Conditioning. Hammer the ends of the stems thoroughly before putting in deep water for an overnight drink. It is best to burn or boil the ends of the young growth. Although privets retain their leaves long after Christmas, it is best not to pick so late, for the foliage will not last well.

Cultivation. Tolerant of any soil conditions, in sun or shade, town or country, privet may be planted from October to April. No pruning is necessary beyond clipping to keep the shrub shapely and in bounds.

Lonicera sempervirens

Lonicera   HONEYSUCKLE

L. japonica 'Aureo-Reticulata', height 25 ft (8 m), spread 10–15 ft (3·4–5 m); *L. periclymenum* 'Belgica', height 15–20 ft (4·5–6 m), spread 10–12 ft (3–4 m); *L. sempervirens*, height 20 ft (6 m), or more.

The scent alone makes the honeysuckle worthy of a corner on the house wall or along a fence. There are so many varieties that it is hard to make a choice. *L. periclymenum*, our wild deciduous honeysuckle, has deliciously scented cream flowers, but I think that *L. periclymenum* 'Belgica', with fragrant deeper red flowers, is better for your garden. *L. japonica*, a striking evergreen Japanese honeysuckle which will climb 30 ft (9 m), has wonderfully fragrant pairs of flowers on long sprays, and scents the air on a July night. It has taken over in areas of the United States, in fact right down the Eastern shore from Connecticut to Florida, and is a real pest; though I have to admit I

thought it a memorable experience to drive through parts of Maryland and Virginia on a warm summer's night where for mile after mile the air was heavily laden with the perfume. *L. japonica* 'Aureo-reticulata' is a variegated form and has become a most popular plant for flower arranging. It climbs well and has long sprays of gold and green paired leaves, turning pinkish in autumn. It is reputed to flower only rarely, though mine, on a north wall, flowers well every year and is most fragrant. *L. sempervirens* has trumpets of scarlet and yellow, and is a most dramatic plant although scentless. I first saw it at Mount Vernon, where it was planted by George Washington, and still flourishes. I came straight back home and ordered it, but to my disappointment find it is too tender for even the most sheltered corner. It may be grown in a cool greenhouse but may reach 20 ft (6 m) or more. In spite of this setback, I find that I now have a honeysuckle of one kind or another blooming for six months in the year.

Arranging. They do not last well in water, but I use and replace daily, as there is generally enough to allow you to do this. Packed into a wooden box in which you have hidden your container, they look attractive, shed their petals on each other, and in this way seem to last better undisturbed. I use trailing sprays when copying arrangements in a Dutch or Flemish painting. The small-leafed 'Aureo-reticulata' provides graceful lines tumbling out of a vase of greens, or of apricot and creams when the leaves are turning colour in the autumn.

Conditioning. Dip the stems into boiling water and then allow them to drink in cool water for an hour. This is especially important when you are using the variegated sprays, as without this treatment they may not last even for one day.

Cultivation. Plant *L. periclymenum* from September to March, *L. japonica* in March or April, *L. sempervirens* in a greenhouse at any time. Honeysuckles are not fussy about soil, but they like a well-drained site, preferably in partial shade, but they will grow in full sun. Pruning consists of thinning out shoots after flowering, and trimming back over vigorous growths in March.

Magnolia

Magnolia grandiflora, height 10–15 ft (3–4·5 m), spread 6–10 ft (2–3 m); *M. liliiflora* 'Nigra', *M.* × *soulangeana*, height 10–20 ft (3–6 m), spread 10–15 ft (3–4·5 m); *M. stellata*, height and spread 8–10 ft (2–3 m); *M. wilsonii*, height 10–15 ft (3–4·5 m), spread 12–15 ft (4–4·5 m).

Magnificent shrubs and trees. Plant now—you haven't a day to lose! I just regret that I will never live to see the best of my magnolias, for I started too late. *M. grandiflora* must be one of the most beautiful trees in the world, with deep green glossy leaves and a burst of enormous creamy white flowers that scent the bedrooms of so many Georgian houses, against which it was often planted. It grows magnificently in the Southern States of America, free standing and beautiful, and I only wish it did as well here. *M.* × *soulangeana*, and the cup-shaped flowers, cream suffused with pink, bloom in spring on bare black branches—a spectacular sight.

'Alba' is a form with pure white flowers; 'Lennei' has magnificent leaves and much larger, tulip-like flowers, rose outside and white within; and 'Rustica Rubra' is a lovely form with the flowers stained a deeper purple. *M. liliiflora*

Magnolia stellata

'Nigra' has large flowers that are deep purple outside, and paler within. *M. stellata* has grey mossy branches and a wealth of white star-like flowers bursting out of furry grey buds in March and April. *M. wilsonii* has nodding blooms with rich red stamens and purplish pistils.

Arranging. A marvellous oriental-type arrangement can be created with a stem of contorted hazel and some magnolia flower heads. Magnolias can be arranged alone, in a mass if you have enough, or one beautiful branch on a shallow dish or in a piece of alabaster—indeed it seems to look right in anything.

Conditioning and preserving. The ends of the stems should be well hammered before being given a long drink. Flowers of the *M. × soulangeana* varieties open well in water if picked when in bud. *M. grandiflora* flowers look spectacular, but do not last well when picked. However, the foliage is superb and lasts for weeks if given fresh water weekly.

To preserve the leaves of *M. grandiflora*, just pick up the fallen bronzy leaves and use them as they are, or coated with a layer of varnish. *M. grandiflora* is a good subject for glycerining: hammer the stems well and put into a solution for several weeks. The leaves will turn a glossy brown and last virtually for ever.

Cultivation. Plant from October to March in any good garden soil, in full sun or partial shade. If possible plant so that the magnolias are sheltered from north and east winds. *M. grandiflora* does best against a south- or west-facing wall. Pruning is not necessary except with *M. grandiflora* grown against a wall where forward-growing shoots must be cut back in spring.

Mahonia

Mahonia aquifolium, height 3–5 ft (1–1·5 m), spread 4–6 ft (1–2 m); *M. bealei*, height and spread 6–8 ft (around 2 m); *M. × 'Charity'*, height 7–10 ft (2–3 m), spread 6–9 ft (2–3 m); *M. japonica*, height 6–10 ft (2–3 m), spread 6–8 ft (1–2·5 m).

One of the best evergreen shrubs, excellent for flower arranging and effective in the garden. The mahonia is sometimes confused with berberis, but is distinguished by its compound leaves and spineless stems. They have handsome pinnate leaves, often with good autumn colour, and yellow flowers. *M. × 'Charity'* and *M. japonica* both have erect racemes of bell flowers and those of *M. japonica* are very sweet-scented: as they start to appear in January, these are particularly welcome. *M. aquifolium*, the Oregon Grape, has good rusty foliage and a wealth of yellow flowers followed by clusters of blue-green berries.

Arranging. Mahonias are good for arranging in leaf, flower or berry stage. I use single leaves of *M. japonica* and *M. × 'Charity'* both at the green stage and, best of all perhaps, in autumn when coloured apricot to scarlet, when they look lovely with dahlias and tawny roses. The small racemes of sweetly scented yellow flowers added to a few *Iris unguicularis* and some early spring bits make delightful small arrangements.

Conditioning and preserving. The woody stems need thorough hammering before being given a long drink. The flowers seem to last a little better if the stem ends are put into $\frac{1}{2}$ in (1.3 cm) of boiling water, and then allowed a long drink.

The individual leaves of *M. japonica* and *M. × 'Charity'* take up glycerine well. Stand them in the solution, and sponge over each leaf with a piece of cotton wool soaked in the solution.

Cultivation. Plant in September or October, or in April or May. Mahonias thrive in sun or partial shade in any good well-drained garden soil. No pruning is normally needed.

Pernettya

P. mucronata 'Alba', 'Davis's Hybrids', 'Lilacina', height and spread 2–3 ft (60–90 cm).

A South American evergreen shrub, a clumpy bush with small leaves and berries in a wonderful range of colours from white and pink to mauve and deep red. Those of *P. mucronata* 'Alba' are white, 'Lilacina' really lilac-coloured and 'Davis's Hybrids' have extra large berries in many colours. They are members of the heath family and enjoy similar conditions.

Philadelphus 'Beauclerk'

Arranging. We have always managed to buy well-berried pernettya branches in Covent Garden, so I have had the opportunity of using them a lot. They look particularly attractive with gentians and autumn crocus, but can be used to add colour and form to any arrangement. Stems of 'Lilacina' are an excellent foil for some of the late mauve roses. If you are picking from your own garden, you may not be able to take long stems, but however short, they tuck into the front of a small vase most effectively.

Conditioning. Put the ends of the stems into a little boiling water and then allow to drink in cool water for an hour or so.

Cultivation. Plant from October to April in a lime free soil. Pernettyas prefer a good rich loamy soil in full sun, although they will put up with light shade. Four or five plants should be planted in a group to ensure pollination and a set of berries. No pruning is normally required, but old leggy plants may be cut back hard in spring.

Philadelphus   'SYRINGA' MOCK ORANGE

Philadelphus 'Beauclerk', height 6–8 ft (around 2 m), spread 5–6 ft (1·5–2 m); *P.* 'Belle Etoile', height 8–10 ft (2·5–3 m), spread 9–12 ft (3–4 m); *P.* 'Burfordiensis', height 8–10 ft (2·5–3 m), spread 9–12 ft (3-4 m); *P.* 'Virginal', height 6–9 ft (2–3 m), spread 6–8 ft (around 2 m); *P. coronarius* 'Aureus', height and spread 6–8 ft (around 2 m).

Often wrongly called syringa, this is a most rewarding deciduous shrub, doing well on poor soils and sending up stems of deliciously sweet-scented white flowers. 'Beauclerk' has large white single flowers with a zone of cerise round the stamens, while the flowers of 'Belle Etoile' are maroon at the centre. 'Burfordiensis' grows up to 10 ft (3 m) in height with straight stems, and is a really lovely single with large open white flowers and a mass of yellow stamens. 'Virginal' is still quoted by every nursery as the best double. One of the best shrubs for golden foliage in spring is *P. coronarius* 'Aureus', bringing a touch of sunlight to any corner of your garden.

Arranging. Stems of philadelphus are invaluable for wedding groups. Once I had the delight of using philadelphus, white delphiniums and white peonies for a wedding in the first week of July, and I feel the result was really ideal. Pieces of *P. coronarius* 'Aureus' make any spring arrangement.

Conditioning. I would strongly recommend you to remove most or even all leaves before you start to condition. If you are using only a few pieces, dip the stem ends in boiling water and then allow a long drink; if you have a great many branches, then plunge them into warm water for a long drink after the stems have been well hammered.

Cultivation. Plant from October to March in sun or partial shade, in any good well-drained garden soil. Pruning consists of cutting out old stems right to the ground after flowering to prevent the bushes from becoming congested.

Photinia

P. serrulata 'Red Robin', height 6 ft (2 m), spread 4–5 ft (1–1·5 m).

This is an evergreen shrub that I have recently become acquainted with but I feel I must mention it as it belongs to such an attractive family. Red Robin has oval leaves and gorgeous dark plum-coloured foliage. It is a sun-lover and does very well in North America, so I am hoping very much that I can manage to keep it.

Arranging. The leaves, through their lovely glossy colour and shape, seem to look good with almost anything. A small piece makes a splendid foil for *Helleborus foetidus*.

Conditioning. The ends of the stems should be put into boiling water and then allowed to have a long drink.

Cultivation. Plant in September or October, or in March or April, in fairly rich loamy soil, in full sun if possible. No pruning is normally required.

Prunus

Prunus cerasifera 'Nigra', height and spread 20–25 ft (6–8 m); *P. communis* 'Pollardii' (now correctly known as *P. dulcis*), height and spread 20–25 ft (6–8 m); *P. davidiana* 'Alba', height 25–30 ft (8–9 m), spread 12–15 ft (4–4·5 m);

P. laurocerasus, height 15–20 ft (4·5–6 m), spread 20–30 ft (6–9 m); *P. lusitanica*, height and spread 15–20 ft (4·5–6 m); *P. padus* 'Watereri' ('Grandiflora'), height 20–25 ft (6–8 m), spread 15–20 ft (4·5–6 m); *P. persica* 'Cardinal', 'Prince Charming', height and spread 15–25 ft (4·5–8 m); *P. serrulata* 'Ukon' ('Grandiflora'), *P. serrulata* 'Amanogawa' ('Erecta'), *P. serrulata* 'Shirotae' ('Kojima'), height 18–25 ft (5–8 m), spread 30–35 ft (9–11 m); *P. subhirtella* 'Autumnalis', 'Pendula Rosea', 'Autumnalis Rosea', height and spread 20–25 ft (6–8 m).

There are so many members of this huge family that I can only suggest a few of my own favourite decorative and fruiting varieties.

A variety of the common almond, *P. communis* 'Pollardii', might be a good one to grow as the flowers are larger than those of the type and of a deeper colour with crimson stamens. The almond is lovely for town gardens, giving a wealth of pink blossom in March, flowering before the leaves on coal black stems. It also forces well, making it a 'must' for the flower arranger.

The flowering peaches I would choose are *P. davidiana* 'Alba', which produces clusters of white flowers on leafless branches in February; *P. persica* 'Cardinal' with vivid double red flowers in April; and *P. persica* 'Prince Charming', with semi-double rosette-like flowers, appearing in April on upright stems.

Flowering plums are also useful for the arranger, especially those with red foliage. *P. cerasifera* 'Nigra' is the improved form of 'Atropurpurea', having darker ruby-red foliage and single pink flowers in March.

P. padus 'Watereri' ('Grandiflora'), the Bird Cherry, flowers later than the other flowering prunus, producing pendulous white racemes in May. This is a wonderful sight in the garden, though sadly short-lived, and is also attractive for arranging.

Among flowering cherries perhaps my favourite is *P. subhirtella* 'Autumnalis', which flowers off and on all winter, starting in November with semi-double white flowers which get pinker with age. I thought I was planting this, but in fact was sent 'Higan-Zakura' (*P. subhirtella* 'Autumnalis Rosea'). I have loved every minute of the deep rose-pink buds in March, which develop into single pink flowers, and it forces well in water.

Prunus subhirtella 'Autumnalis'

flora') with bronzy young foliage, and greenish flowers which turn creamy-buff after opening.

P. lusitanica, Portugal laurel, has bay-like leaves and pendulous white flowers in June. It is a good evergreen, even hardier than the common laurel, *P. laurocerasus*. The latter has good shiny oval leaves of pale green turning darker as they mature, white flowers and purple berries. It is a good shrub for sunless areas.

Arranging. Sprays of delicate pink almond blossoms on dark stems can be forced as early as February. A month later, it can be picked in the garden and used as background for a few blue iris and pink hyacinths or tulips, or added to a few bought flowers to make a delightful arrangement. *P. subhirtella* 'Autumnalis', flowering all winter, can be used with the first *Iris unguicularis*, or twigs placed to give height to a moss garden of crocus, snowdrops and aconites. The purple-leaved plums, though difficult to condition, are wonderful background material for a vase of pink rhododendrons and purple lilacs. 'Ukon', in the first stages of opening buds, looks so good with greens, or in a vase of contrasting purples—dark tulips and early peonies. All these flowering trees must be picked with great care, but even the weeping varieties need a little pruning or shaping every now and then, so trim them when you want branches for forcing, or later when the trees are in flower, so that you can shape the tree and have material for flower arranging at the same time.

Leaves of the common and Portugal laurel make excellent backgrounds for large church groups, especially on a windowsill where you can have a problem screening the light so that it doesn't take all the colour. Stems of laurel also look well when the leaves are browned in glycerine, either in a vase of dried material, or with fresh evergreens, in both cases providing solid contrast of form. The fruits of any of the plum or peach families should be used on the branch, or for fruit and flower arrangements like those in early flower paintings.

Conditioning and preserving. All woody stems need careful treatment. Either hammer the ends, stripping off the bark for about 3 in (7·5 cm) up the stem, or dip the stem ends in boiling water. In both cases follow by a long drink.

P. subhirtella 'Pendula Rosea' (Cheal's Weeping Cherry) has long branches sweeping to the ground which in April are covered with small pink flowers. All weeping trees are decorative, particularly in flower, but though suitable in many ways for a small garden, they need to be planted in a lawn, where their beauty can be really appreciated. The most wonderful specimen of 'Pendula Rosea' I have ever seen was in Portland, Oregon; it must have stood 30 ft (9 m) high and was smothered in superb cascading pink blossom.

Other good Japanese cherries are hybrids from *P. serrulata*: *P. serrulata* 'Amanogawa' ('Erecta') Lombardy Poplar Cherry, with clusters of semi-double pale pink flowers, becoming a veritable pillar of flower, is ideal for the small garden. The widely planted 'Kanzan' (*P. serrulata* 'Sekiyama') I could well do without, as I think there are better ones to grow, such as 'Shirotae' ('Kojima'), with large pendulous flowers on beautifully shaped arching branches; or 'Ukon' (*P. serrulata* 'Grandi-

The only member of the prunus family that will preserve well is the common laurel. After picking, give the branches a drink of warm water, so that the leaves are really crisp. Then stand in 1 in (2·5 cm) of glycerine and hot water solution, and you will see the leaves gradually turning brown. To help them take up the solution more quickly paint a little glycerine on to the leaves with cotton wool. You should allow anything up to four weeks for this process.

Cultivation. Plant from October to March in any well-drained reasonably fertile garden soil, preferably in full sun or light shade. If the soil is slightly alkaline, this is an advantage. All the prunus family is rather shallow rooted, and the trees should be firmly staked for the first few years after planting.

No regular pruning is normally needed on the almonds, peaches, plums or cherries, but the ordinary laurel and the Portuguese laurel may be cut back with secateurs to keep them within bounds. Old specimens that have become bare at the base may be cut hard back to 1–2 ft (30–60 cm) above ground and they will make new growth.

Pyracantha   FIRETHORN

Pyracantha angustifolia, height 10 ft (3 m), spread 6–8 ft (around 2 m); *P. crenulata* 'Rogersiana', *P. crenulata* 'Rogersiana Flava', height 8–10 ft (2·5–3 m), spread 10–15 ft (3–4·5 m).

Handsome shrubs with masses of white flowers in spring and a profusion of orange or yellow berries in late summer. They are generally used for training against a wall or fence, and can reach up to 8 or 9 ft (around 2·6 m) or more. The berries of *P. angustifolia* are particularly fine, and if not taken by the birds will last right into winter and may even still be there in spring. *P. crenulata* 'Rogersiana', has deeper red berries and can be trained to grow on a wall or as a bush in the open. 'Flava' is the variety I personally prefer, as the berries are a bright clear yellow.

Arranging. As the stems grow pretty tall, one can use berried branches 4 or 5 ft (around 1·4 m) long, making them ideal for a church group or really large arrangements. The yellow-berried form tones in well with yellow flowers like dahlias, roses and gladioli, whereas the orange-berried branches make a marvellous background for apricot and orange flowers and any arrangement of good autumnal colours. I once used the red-berried form in Santiago with *Strelitzia reginae* and a collection of succulents in deep russet colours, and even with all these tropical exotics, the Firethorn made a wonderful contribution to the arrangement.

Conditioning. Hammer the woody stems very hard and allow several hours in warm water before arranging.

Cultivation. Plant October to March in full sun or partial shade in any good garden soil; they will put up with some lime in the soil. They make excellent wall plants, but must be tied to wires or square-mesh wire panels until they can stand on their own. If grown as bushes in the open no pruning is required, but if grown against a wall or fence they should be trimmed as necessary in early summer.

Rhododendron

'Christmas Cheer', 'Cunningham's White', 'Doncaster', 'Pink Pearl', height and spread 6–10 ft (2–3 m); 'Praecox', 'Purple Splendour', height and spread 3–4 ft (around 1 m).

These familiar evergreen shrubs with large leaves and clustered flower heads range from small rock varieties to massive plants growing up to 30 ft (9 m), all equally attractive and effective in their own way. The hybrid rhododendrons have beautiful foliage, felty and brown backed, and some are sweet-scented with nodding bells. They can be grown from seed if you are patient, and it is also possible to move them at almost any age. I have chosen 'Doncaster' as a good red; 'Pink Pearl' as one of the handsomest of all with large heads of deep to paler pink flowers; 'Cunningham's White' as a good early white; 'Christmas Cheer' as a very early pink; and 'Praecox' as a very early delicate flowered mauve. These last two early varieties are particularly helpful for the flower arranger, though also effective in the garden.

Arranging. Christmas Cheer' deserves its name, as the early blooms can be used in a Christmas arrangement with bergenia flowers, hyacinths and *Iris unguicularis*. I use a piece of 'Praecox' with blue and pink hyacinths. The larger varieties make splendid centres for any large arrangement, though it is advisable to remove some of the green leaves as these can cover the flower heads. Used like this, they are invaluable for the flower arranger, and I am always sad when their season ends.

Conditioning and preserving. The ends of the stems should be hammered, or dipped in boiling water (I prefer this second method). Remove some of the foliage, not only to show the face, but because the flowers will last longer. I was once given a tip to add a little household bleach to the water, and it certainly seems to help keep the flowers fresh.

The foliage of rhododendron glycerines well, going a good brown colour. The seed heads of some of the hybrids also dry well.

Cultivation. These rhododendrons must have an acid soil. They will thrive in light shade and need shelter from north and east winds. They are very shallow rooted and need plenty of water on quick-draining soils in dry spells. Plant from October to March. No pruning is required but old gaunt specimens may be cut back hard. It is better however, to replace such worn-out shrubs, or move them to a better place if they are too big for their present position.

Ribes FLOWERING CURRANT

Ribes laurifolium, height and spread 12–18 in (30–45 cm); *R. sanguineum* 'Atrorubens', 'Brocklebank', 'Carneum', height 6–9 ft (2–3 m), spread 5–8 ft (1·5–2·5 m).

Flowering currants are good for both planting and arranging, whether the prostrate *R. laurifolium*, with masses of greenish-white flowers in February, or the better-known *R. sanguineum*. Here I would recommend 'Atrorubens', a North American variety with deepest red flowers, 'Brocklebank', worthy of a place for its golden foliage and pink flowers, and 'Carneum' with flesh-pink flowers.

Arranging. Currants can be forced so easily that they are worth growing for that alone. Early forced stems, mixed with a bunch of bought pale tulips or some lilies, bring a feeling of spring and blossom time very early in the year.

Conditioning. To force, pick branches as the buds are forming, hammer the stems well and place in warm water. If you can stand them in a dark place they seem to come out much more quickly. They need about five weeks to bloom, and the forced flowers are much paler than those grown out of doors, but are none the less attractive.

For branches picked when in blossom, dip the stem ends into boiling water and then allow a long drink before using.

Cultivation. Plant October to March in any good garden soil in an open sunny site, or even in light shade. No pruning is normally necessary, but old worn-out stems should be cut out at the base in spring.

Rosa ROSE

Shrub roses, height 5–6 ft (1·5–2 m), spread 4–6 ft (1–2 m); Hybrid tea roses, height 3–4 ft (around 1 m), spread 2–3 ft (60–90 cm); Floribundas, height 3–4 ft (around 1 m), spread 2–3 ft (60–90 cm); Climbing roses, height and spread normally 10–15 ft (3–4·5 m).

What an impossible task it is to choose a collection of roses! Once again, I can only list a few of my favourites in each group, but for anyone trying to make their own selection I would recommend going to look at them in bloom first. The Rose Trial Grounds at St Albans are well worth a visit for this reason alone.

Shrub roses. If you have enough space, shrub roses are rewarding to grow for their fantastic scents and old-fashioned charm, and though for arranging they are not to be compared with the modern Hybrid teas, they last quite well if displayed in a mass. I am not going to attempt to give details of parentage or full Latin names, but simply list my selection according to their colour.

A pure white is 'Blanc Double de Coubert', flowering over a long period, even though individual flowers are short-lived.

In the purple to violet group: 'Charles de Mills',

Rose 'Peace'

Spry' is a modern shrub rose, and I think one of the best of all, with large pink flowers, a musky scent and a wealth of bloom for two weeks or more. I find that it grows with great vigour if trained against a wall. Crosses from 'Constance Spry', such as 'Chaucer', are also well worth trying.

Hybrid teas. White: 'Message', 'Pascali', 'Virgo', 'John F. Kennedy' if you can find it in this country. It is a superb greenish-white, and I have used it in both America and Australia.

The best cream rose is undoubtedly 'Elizabeth Harkness'.

Clear yellows: 'Sunblest', 'King's Ransom', 'Miss Harp', 'Golden Times'.

Apricot colourings: 'Whisky Mac', 'Bettina', 'Apricot Silk', 'Beauté'.

Reds: 'Ena Harkness' and 'Josephine Bruce' for velvet red roses; 'Christian Dior', 'Super Star', 'Fragrant Cloud', 'Eroica', 'Sir Harry Pilkington'.

Pinks: 'Lady Helen', 'Anne Letts', 'Northern Lights'—and for me 'Ophelia' takes a lot of beating.

Mauve to purples: 'Blue Moon', 'Sterling Silver', 'Lilac Time'.

Off-beat colours: 'Helen Traubel', pinkish-apricot and one of the earliest to flower; 'Iced

richest deep purple to mauve; 'Cardinal de Richelieu', deep violet; the striped 'Variegata di Bologna', purple and white.

'Tuscany' has maroon-coloured velvety petals with a cluster of yellow stamens. The semi-climber 'Madame Isaac Pereire' has heavily scented deep magenta pink flowers, and is a lovely rose for arrangements.

The largest group is of pink-flowered roses, from among the oldest to very recent introductions. A variety of the White Rose of Yorkshire is 'Great Maiden's Blush', known since the fifteenth century and so vigorous that it is still found today. 'Celeste' is another member of the same family, with a wealth of soft pink blooms. 'Madame Lauriol de Barny' has flat heads of many-petalled pink flowers, and 'Fantin Latour' also has handsome foliage. 'Madame Pierre Oger' is better known as the Shell Rose, and has creamy pink flowers that deepen with age. 'Constance

Opposite
1 Hyacinth
2 Erica

Toning colours of mauve, pink, blue and white form the basis of this spring arrangement of mixed hyacinths and ericas. The flowers spill out of their container, a brass-edged wooden tea caddy, which has a liner inside to hold water.

'Ginger', light tan-coloured; 'Fantan', brownish; 'Amber', light golden brown and buff; 'Jocelyn', purple brown and most unusual. Lastly, 'Pink Chiffon', delicate pink buds with deeper pink centres.

Floribundas. 'Iceberg' must be the top favourite, a pure white. 'Elizabeth of Glamis', 'Sir Lancelot' and 'Apricot Nectar' are good apricot shades. 'Fashion' is deep salmon. 'Woburn Abbey' orange and gold—all these orangey colours perhaps even more useful in the autumn than in high summer. Good reds are 'Lilli Marlene', 'Topsy', 'Ginger Megg' and 'Rosemary Rose', though this last one does suffer from mildew.

Climbing roses. I have included *Rosa filipes* 'Kifsgate' here for growing over an old apple or pear tree, or to smother an unsightly shed. It is at

Opposite
1 Iris
2 Euphorbia
3 Wallflower
4 Auricula
5 *Bellis perennis* ~~english daisy~~
6 Forget-me-not
7 Rhododendron
8 Auricula ~~primula (primrose)~~

The yellows and pinks of wallflowers, auriculas, *bellis perennis*, irises and rhododendrons pick up the warm colouring of this unusual terracotta basket which was made in Florida. The absence of green in the arrangement intensifies the bright effect.

its peak in July, producing a mass of very sweetly scented white flower sprays with yellow stamens. Another lovely species rose is *R. banksiae* 'Lutea', with double rosette flowers of soft buttercup yellow, very sweet scented and needing little pruning. It is found on many old houses, and I am only sorry that I did not plant it myself many years ago. 'Mermaid' is particularly desirable for its superb glossy green foliage and because it flowers for such a long period, from June to November, producing its single yellow open flowers with amber stamens. 'Paul's Lemon Pillar' is one of the earliest roses to come out and its creamy yellow flowers are doubly welcome for this reason. 'Climbing All-gold' is an excellent yellow with a long blooming period and good dark-green foliage. 'Albertine' is not for the small garden as its rampant growth would take you over very quickly, and it needs a lot of attention to keep it in shape, but you are rewarded with a wealth of reddish buds opening to pale salmon pink, and with a perfume that wafts into every corner of the house on a warm June night.

For reds there is nothing to beat 'Guinée' with dark rich colour and wonderful scent, or 'Etoile de Holland', not such a deep red but an old and popular rose still to be recommended. 'New Dawn' looks like an old rose but was actually hybridized in 1930 in New Jersey. It is excellent for climbing over an old tree, and its pale pink beautifully shaped flowers are most useful for arranging.

Arranging. I still never cease to be amazed at the great gasp that goes up whenever I show a slide of a mass of pink roses during a lecture. Roses are one of the few flowers that most of us can arrange *en masse*, for it is usually possible to pick quite a lot at one time. On the other hand they are the ideal focal point and centre for so many arrangements, and I sometimes find myself wondering what to put into the middle of a vase when there are no roses in bloom, even being tempted to buy some, however expensive, to provide that final touch. Only the single blooms of climbing roses such as 'Mermaid' will not last well in arrangements. In mixed arrangements, I think roses can be used to best effect where they provide contrast in colour and form (such as a few white roses in a green and white arrangement, or roses for the white emphasis in a near-black and white arrangement) and where they are used as focal points in arrangements of many shades of one colour (such as mixed reds in high summer; or apricot colourings in autumn with turning leaves, apricot dahlias and gladioli). **Conditioning and preserving.** Dip the stem ends in boiling water for a minute, then follow with a long drink in cold water for several hours. Or hammer the ends of the stems and then give them a long drink in warm water.

It is possible to treat these flowers so that you can have them in bloom at Christmas: pick when the roses are in bud, wax the ends of the stems with paraffin wax and lay them in a long, closed cardboard box until Christmas. Then cut off the wax ends and place the stems in warm water: you will find that they open up very well.

Buds and even fully blown roses can be preserved in silica gel. Remove the stem and insert a florist's wire in its place (the stem would just break off when dry), then lay the rose face upwards on a bed of powder. Sprinkle with more powder, taking care to fill every crevice, until the bloom is completely covered. Leave for a few days before testing to see if the petals are perfectly dry and crisp.

Dried rose petals make wonderful potpourri. They should be spread on trays to dry out of doors, but not in full sun.

Cultivation. Plant October to March. Roses prefer a sunny open site and will thrive in any good well-drained soil. On light soils work in plenty of peat or organic manure, and feed well with a soluble fertilizer every year.

Pruning of established roses: shrub roses need only shortening back of the main stems by a few inches, and any old worn-out stems cut out at ground level in March. Hybrid tea roses are pruned in December, or at any time when growth is dormant, up to March. Cut out weak and worn-out shoots. Cut main shoots back to leave about five or six buds or eyes. Cut to just above an outward pointing bud. Floribunda roses are also pruned from December to March, but more lightly pruned. Cut back weak shoots to

leave three or four buds, but on strong growths leave five to seven buds. Climbing roses are pruned after flowering. If there are sufficient new growths to take their place, cut out completely the older stems. Bend the new growths over as nearly horizontal as possible to encourage the production of side shoots which will bear the flowers in the next year.

Salix   WILLOW

Salix alba 'Chermesina' ('Britzensis'), height 30–40 ft (9–12 m), spread 15–25 ft (4.5–8 m); *S. babylonica*, height 20–25 ft (6–8 m), spread 20–30 ft (6–9 m); *S. lanata*, height 2–4 ft (60 cm–1.2 m), spread 1–4 ft (30 cm–1.2 m); *S. matsudana* 'Tortuosa', height 20–30 ft (6–9 m), spread 10–15 ft (3–4.5 m).

A vast range of plants from tiny shrubs suitable for a rock garden to large trees such as S. *babylonica*, the weeping willow. This is a very decorative tree, much taller than our native pussy willow, with very graceful hanging branches, bright yellow in spring. It looks particularly lovely underplanted with daffodils. But it is not a tree for the small garden, and is one that can be difficult, too, in built-up areas, as willows have a way of looking for water, and their roots can cause havoc while in pursuit of it. S. *lanata* is indigenous to Scotland, where I found mine, and makes a handsome small shrub of 2–3 ft (60–90 cm), with silver-grey fluffy down on the leaves, stems and golden yellow catkins. S. *matsudana* 'Tortuosa', the fan-tail willow, is wonderful for arrangements, with corkscrew-twisted red fasciated stems edged with silver catkins. S. 'Britzensis' to use its familiar name, has lovely red bark in winter, and when brought into the house the catkins open well in water.

Arranging. The weeping willow is the only one that does not last well in water. I have used it for a wedding group, where the tumbling yellow stems were ideal, but it lived for just one day. All other willows last well and are a joy for winter and early spring as they develop in water. I use the 'Tortuosa' willow a great deal as it has such an excellent form for oriental-type arrangements. Small stems of native pussy willow (*S. caprea*) look well in spring arrangements with hellebores.

Conditioning and preserving. Hammer the ends of the stems and then put into warm water. For forcing, follow this procedure, but keep the branches in the dark for the first few days. Pussy willow stems will dry off in shallow water and can be used all winter.

Cultivation. Plant from October to March in any soil. All willows love moist conditions, so the tall trees are not suitable for small gardens or dry soils. A fully grown willow can transpire a ton of water a day and thus rob a large area of ground of moisture.

No pruning is required for the larger trees, but those grown for their coloured stems should be cut down almost to ground level in January or February every year.

Symphoricarpos   SNOWBERRY

S. albus 'Laevigatus' (*S. rivularis*), height 5–7 ft (1·5–2 m), spread 7–8 ft (around 2 m).

Snowberries will grow in the shade, though I found that mine did much better in full sun, making 2–3 ft (60–90 cm) bushes of small-leaved plants with insignificant flowers followed by round white berries which are so pretty, and stay

Symphoricarpos albus 'White Hedger'

on the bush until after Christmas. There are pink-berried forms, and I have cut these in America but never used them here.

Arranging. If you can cut stems of about 6 in (15 cm) long, they fall gracefully from the centre of an arrangement. They are ideal with black privet berries, late-flowering 'Iceberg' roses and small white dahlias, to make an unusual black and white arrangement.

Conditioning. The stems need little treatment, but are better if left in deep water for some hours. They will last for weeks in water provided you take care to remove any brown and dying berries, for once started the rot seems to spread very quickly.

Cultivation. Plant October to March in any reasonably good soil, in sun or shade, even under the drip of trees. Birds seldom take the berries unless they are desperate. No pruning is normally needed beyond thinning out overcrowding branches, which may be done during the autumn or winter.

Syringa   LILAC

S. vulgaris (single and double varieties), height 8–12 ft (2·5–4 m), spread 6–10 ft, (2–3 m); Preston hybrids, height and spread 8–10 ft (2·5–3 m).

I can never bring myself to talk about lilac as syringa, which of course it is! With its beauty and scent it is undoubtedly a 'must' for every garden. The singles are my favourites: the 'Primrose' lilac has heads of beautiful cream flowers, while 'Maud Notcutt' is an excellent single white. 'Massena' is a well-scented deep purple, and 'Souvenir de Louis Spath' is another with a deep wine colour and heavily clustered heads. For the doubles 'Charles Joly' is dark purple, 'Edward J. Gardner' a light pink, and 'Mrs Edward Harding' is a good red. 'Madame Lemoine' is to my way of thinking the best double white. The Preston hybrids are lovely with their delicate colours, but they are hard to condition for the house. Lilacs need a cold period in the year and do not do well on the west coast of America, though I heard a story of one wealthy lady who, being determined

Syringa 'Miss Ellen Willmott'

seed heads as flowers fade. Remove suckers using a sucker cutter to chop off the sucker below ground where it leaves the roots. Thin out weak shoots that may clutter up the bush. Old bushes bare low down may be cut hard back to 3 ft (1 m) above ground to encourage new growths.

Viburnum

Viburnum × bodnantense, height 9–10 ft (around 3 m), spread 8–12 ft. (2·5–4 m); *V. × burkwoodii*, height 7–8 ft (around 2 m), spread 8–12 ft (2–4 m); *V. carlesii*, height and spread 4–5 ft (1–1·5 m); *V. fragrans*, height and spread 9–12 ft (3–4 m); *V. opulus* 'Sterile', height and spread 15 ft (4·5 m); *V. tinus*, height 6–10 ft (2–3 m), spread 6–7 ft (around 2 m); *V. tomentosum*, height 8–10 ft (2–3 m), spread 10–15 ft (3–4·5 m).

A varied and extensive family, from which I have selected just a few. *V. × burkwoodii* is a very attractive evergreen shrub growing to about 5 ft (1·5 m) with rounded clusters of pink flowers, sweetly scented, appearing from January to April. The deciduous *V. carlesii* is rather similar in appearance, but with looser heads of flowers, pink in bud and opening to white in April and May. *V. fragrans* is one of my favourite deciduous shrubs because I can pick its scented pink blossoms from autumn through to next spring. *V. opulus* 'Sterile', the deciduous Guelder Rose or Snowball Tree, has rounded hanging globes of bright green flowers, turning white as they develop, and leaves with good autumn colouring. *V. tinus*, evergreen and growing up to 10 ft (3 m), exists in many varieties and is another useful winter-flowering plant, by March covered in pinky-white blossom. The wide-spreading horizontal branches of *V. tomentosum* give this beautiful oriental shrub its characteristic appearance, flowering along the top of the branches and with beautiful deeply-veined leaves. The deciduous *V. × bodnantense* is another I cannot leave out, as the deep pink flowers in winter are a joy both to look at in the garden and to arrange for the house.

Arranging. As these are all shrubs of merit, you will have to pick with care, and the length of stem will be determined by your tree. I cannot resist taking little pieces of all the sweetly scented ones and using them for small arrangements. You can

to grow them in the West, had a trench dug each autumn and filled it with ice to give the lilac roots the conditions they needed. So, if you are keen enough, you can somehow manage to grow anything anywhere!

Arranging. Nothing looks more luscious and wonderful than a large vase of lilac which fills the house with scent. White lilac is a great asset for a large white group for a wedding, and the purples blend in with rhododendrons, mixed lupins and delphiniums for a glorious summer arrangement.

Conditioning. It is best to remove much of the foliage, for the stems do not seem able to take up enough water for both the flower and foliage on the same branch. So remove most of the leaves and use a stem of green leaves separately. Peel off the bark to about 2 in (5 cm) up the stem, but be sure that all the white part of the stem is well under the water line or it will die. Then place the ends of the stems in boiling water and leave in deep water overnight for the best results.

Cultivation. Plant from October to March in sun or light shade, in any good garden soil. Remove cut more lavishly from *V. opulus* 'Sterile' as heavy pruning seems to improve it. When the leaves are removed the lime-green snowball flowers are revealed, and it is at this stage that I like them best, especially for an arrangement copying a Flemish flower painting, with striped tulips and lilac. After the leaves of this viburnum have turned colour, I use them a great deal, as I find they last better than any other autumn-tinted foliage.

Conditioning and preserving. All the sweet-scented varieties should have their stems dipped in boiling water and be given a few hours in deep water. For some reason the flowers of *V. carlesii* do not last well, but I love their scent so much that I pick one piece at a time and replace daily if necessary. The stems of *V. opulus* 'Sterile' should be hammered.

The deeply veined leaves of *V. tomentosum* take up glycerine extremely well.

Cultivation. Plant October to March in any good garden soil, preferably not too sandy or quick draining. Viburnums do best in an open sunny site. They do not need much pruning beyond thinning out old worn-out shoots and generally keeping the plants shapely.

Vitis VINE
Ampelopsis VIRGINIA CREEPER

Vitis vinifera, V. vinifera 'Purpurea', height 20 ft (6 m), spread 10–15 ft (3–4·5 m); *Ampelopsis aconitifolia*, height 20 ft (6 m), spread 10–15 ft (3–4·5 m).

Under this heading I have grouped one true vine, *V. vinifera* 'Purpurea', and one Virginia Creeper, *Ampelopsis aconitifolia*, because they both have superb autumn colour and are useful for the flower arranger. The large leaves of *A. aconitifolia* are most ornamental in autumn, changing from pink to glowing scarlet. The leaves of *V. vinifera* 'Purpurea' are a good purple colour all year, but deepen in autumn, and this plant produces the most lovely bunches of maroon-coloured grapes, which makes it doubly useful.

Arranging. The large leaves of *A. aconitifolia* do not last long once they have changed colour, but they are wonderful to use for some special occasion. Sprays can give a big group of autumn colour a special touch of drama that is hard to beat. I use individual leaves for fruit and flower groups in my own home.

Small bunches of purple grapes from *V. vinifera* 'Purpurea' and a few trails of its maroon leaves are quite lovely with some full-blown red roses.

Conditioning and preserving. The stems of both subjects last better if dipped in boiling water and then submerged overnight, or at least for a few hours.

Both leaves may be given the wax treatment: iron with a cool iron between wax paper, then add false stems made with florist's wire.

Cultivation. Plant from October to March in any reasonably good soil. A west- or south-facing aspect against a wall is best, especially for the vine if grapes are to be produced. The ampelopsis needs no pruning. The vitis may need to have surplus growths removed in early spring and some of the lush shoots pinched back in early summer.

Wistaria

Wistaria sinensis, W. sinensis 'Alba', height up to 80–100 ft (24–50 m).

Quite the best and most popular wistaria is *W. sinensis*, and a wall smothered with the long mauve racemes of sweet-scented flowers looks magnificent—though since visiting the gardens at Bodnant I confess I have bitterly regretted not planting the white variety, *W. sinensis* 'Alba'. It is one of the most beautiful sights I have ever seen.

Arranging. Wistarias are not long-lived in water, but nevertheless are worth picking as you will usually have plenty, and each stem can therefore be replaced easily. Just a branch of twisted willow (*Salix matsudana* 'Tortuosa') and a stem of wistaria takes a lot of beating: so simple but very effective. One of the prettiest arrangements I ever made was a vase of pale pink peonies, 'Nellie Moser' clematis and mauve wistaria, which added a luscious touch that is hard to describe.

Conditioning. I always wrap the flower trusses in tissue paper, then dip the stem ends in really boiling water for a count of twenty, followed by the usual long drink in deep water. The tissue paper protects the tender blooms from the steam. In Japan I gather that they keep a bottle of pure spirit and allow the stems to drink that for a few hours before arranging.

Cultivation. Plant from October to March in any good garden soil. Wistarias will ramble up over trees; they can be trained against a wall or over a porch or pergola; or they can be grown as a free-standing bush. They prefer a sunny aspect.

Against a wall or as a free-standing bush all new shoots must be pinched back when they have made four leaves in summer. Then in winter these shoots should be pruned back to leave only two buds.

Perennials & Ground Cover

How many of these plants you can grow will depend very much on the space you have available. They are all useful, dual-purpose plants—they pick well and are valuable for house decoration as well as being attractive while growing. Euphorbias, hellebores and hostas are a 'must'; all have a good form when growing, and when picked give a wide range of colour and a variety of shapes for arrangements. They need to be planted in blocks in the garden to obtain the best effect. Nowadays we have learnt a lot about the visual effect of block colouring, planting three or four plants of the same variety together as they might be placed in an arrangement. When you are planting several flowers together it doesn't matter if they are not of the same variety provided they have the same colouring. Never hesitate to use blocks of greens and greys—in any border these restful zones are essential and give increased effectiveness to the colours of the flower blocks. Follow the same principles when interplanting shrubs or the herbaceous border with perennials.

Finally, there are now so many plants with variegated leaf colours that it is important to bear in mind that the colours and shapes of massed leaves can be just as effective as a bed of annuals, colourful though they are.

Acanthus

Acanthus mollis, *A. spinosus*, height 3–4 ft (around 1 m), planting distance 2–3 ft (60–90 cm).

Acanthus grows well in full sun or shade, making it a worthwhile plant for any fair-sized garden, with handsome foliage and tall flower spikes, purplish with distinct white under-petals.

Arranging. I love to use the long flower stems, but as these are generally 3–4 ft (around 1 m) in height, they are only suitable for large arrangements, for cutting the stems short would destroy the beautiful proportions. They make an excellent background for a large group of mixed flowers in midsummer. The arrangement in the English delftware jar on page 133 is a very good example of how the rounded heads of agapanthus and hydrangea are enhanced by the pointed structural value of the acanthus spikes. Sadly, the beautifully decorative leaves do not last well in water.

Conditioning and preserving. Flower stems should be picked when the florets are open right up the stem: if picked with unopened buds, the stems tend to flop over and rarely recover. The stem ends should be dipped in boiling water followed by a long drink in deep cold water for several hours. Try as I may, I cannot get young leaves to hold up in water; better results can sometimes be achieved with mature leaves, if the stem ends are dipped in boiling water and then submerged completely in cold water, or, better still, a weak solution of starch.

The flower spikes dry well for winter use. I have found the most successful way is to allow them to dry off in the vase in which they are arranged. If this is not possible, they can be hung upside down to dry in a warm room.

Cultivation. Plant in a sunny or semi-shaded spot, from October to March. Any good garden soil is suitable. Cut the flower stems down to ground level after flowering.

Achillea YARROW

Achillea filipendulina 'Gold Plate', height 4 ft (1·2 m), spread 2 ft (60 cm).

The gold-coloured flat heads and the stiff stems with attractive fern-like leaves make a splendid long-lasting show in the border and provide excellent material for the flower arranger.

Arranging. Though I use these heads freshly cut, for me achillea is invaluable when dried and used in winter as it keeps such a good colour. It is effective with yellow mixed flowers in summer and looks well in the centre of a mixed foliage arrangement. The flat heads should always be placed so that they face you as they make a marvellous focal point in any display. They last superbly—a joy in summer when so many flowers shed their petals. They can be used on short stems of 2 in (5 cm), or full length up to 4 ft (1·2 cm).

Conditioning and preserving. The flowers last well with no special treatment. Though the stalks can be hung upside down to dry, I prefer to stand them in a jug in a little warm water, making sure the heads are not touching. They dry quickly like this and keep their shape. Covering the heads with borax gives a little better colour, but you may think, as I do, that it is hardly worth the extra trouble.

Cultivation. Plant from October to March in any good well-drained garden soil. Achilleas like full sun. Cut the stems down to ground level in the general autumn clearing up.

Aconitum lycoctonum MONKSHOOD

Height 4½ ft (1·3 m), planting distance 3 ft (1 m).

The more common varieties of monkshood have blue-mauve flower spikes resembling those of a delphinium, but the one I would like to recommend here is *A. lycoctonum*, very delicate in form with yellowish to lime-green flowers. To be fair, I feel that this is a plant for the larger garden, as it really takes up quite a lot of space and flowers for a comparatively short time—and also really needs staking. However, as this is a book about flowers

that I would like to have in the garden and for arranging, I am anxious to include it here.

Arranging. It is lovely to mix with a group of yellow and white flowers, and I find that one or two stems really add so much to a small mixed summer flower arrangement. The seed heads are pretty whether used when green or allowed to dry completely, turning brown.

Conditioning and preserving. Give a long drink in deep warm water. The seed heads dry well if hung upside down in a warm place.

Cultivation. This is a hardy perennial, easily raised from seed. It will grow in any good garden soil in sun or partial shade. Cut the old stems down to ground level in the autumn.

Opposite
1 Viburnum
2 Hyacinth
3 Narcissus
4 Forsythia
5 Polyanthus
6 Prunus × 'Pandora'

An informal spring display of narcissi, forsythia, pink and blue hyacinths, pink cherry blossom and viburnum foliage arranged in a pewter jug. Jugs are always suitable for the less formal arrangement.

Overleaf
A mass of one type of flower, arranged quite simply. The rich, contrasting colours of polyanthuses look dramatic with their own foliage in this gold vase.

Agapanthus

Headbourne Hybrids, height 2–3 ft (60–90 cm), planting distance 2 ft (60 cm).

These are the best hybrids of this increasingly popular plant. Carrying round heads of clustered florets on stout, smooth stems that grow 2–3 ft (60–90 cm) high, they are most welcome for the flower arranger as they give a blue flower head at a time when there are few other tall blue flowers. I have always felt that agapanthus was not hardy,

Page 69
1 *Cornus mas*
2 Iris
3 Hellebore
4 Leucojum *lummer Snowdrop*
5 *Bellis perennis*
6 *Scilla tubergeniana*
7 Tellima
8 Ivy berries

This delicate, modern Italian cupid vase highlights the graceful lines of an arrangement of mixed hellebores, irises, leucojum and *bellis perennis*. The rich, dark tellima foliage and the black ivy berries make a good background to a predominantly green and pink group of flowers.

Opposite
A two-tier stand which is useful at many times during the year but which looks its best with mixed sprays of pink and white flowering cherry blossom.

but today there seem to be several hardy strains. Whether grown against a wall, or in the herbaceous or shrub border, they provide a lovely patch of blue and a nice change of form, with their decorative strap-like basal leaves.

Arranging. I think one of the best examples of the use of agapanthus can be seen in the arrangement with acanthus in the delftware jar on page 133, though they will mix well in any large arrangement, using the stems short or full length. They add that vital touch of blue so important in mixed flower groups, or make an excellent focal point for a foliage arrangement in late July through to September, the combination of blue colour and rounded shape making an excellent foil against mixed leaves.

Conditioning and preserving. The flower heads last very well with no special treatment but, rather like azaleas, it is important to remove each floret as it dies, or the whole head begins to look dead long before it is really over. The buds continue to open in water, so you can keep the flower stems in a vase for a few weeks.

For preserving, leave the flower heads on the stems until the seed is well formed, then cut and hang the stems upside down to dry off thoroughly. They can then be used whole, or taken apart and used individually in smaller vases.

Cultivation. Plant in April or May in any good garden soil, but preferably against a south- or west-facing wall. It is a worthwhile precaution to protect the plants against winter frosts by covering them in October or November with a 6 in (15 cm) layer of peat, straw or bracken.

Alchemilla mollis

Height 12–18 in (30–45 cm), planting distance 15 in (40 cm).

Without any doubt alchemilla is a 'must' for every garden, with its lime-green or sulphury-yellow feathery sprays of flower, which I use continuously from June to August. The flower stems branch from compact umbels of cup-like leaves which, because of their silky hairs, retain rain drops to glitter like quicksilver after showers.

Alchemilla mollis

Arranging. Because of the delicate form and wonderful blending colour of the flowers, I am tempted to use alchemilla in almost all my arrangements. It lasts so well, and adds such a soft touch that I look forward to it flowering, and it is a joy to find a piece that has blossomed in late autumn. The colour mixes well with pinks, reds, blues, yellows and of course any all-green arrangement.

Conditioning and drying. It really needs no special treatment, but it is best to remove a few of the leaves, as these tend to die long before the flower, and then give the stems a long drink in deep water. Remove all foliage.

The flower dries well, though naturally loses some colour. Drying is best done by allowing stems to dry off in the vase in which they are arranged.

Cultivation. Plant from October to March in any good well-drained soil, in sun or partial shade. Twiggy sticks may be needed to support the plants if they are growing strongly. Cut almost to ground level in the autumn. A moisture-lover, it does not do well in hot and dry areas.

Alstroemeria

Alstroemeria ligtu hybrids, height 3 ft (1 m), planting distance 12–15 in (30–40 cm).

The ligtu hybrids are the only alstroemerias that I personally would consider growing. Once established, they will reward you with a profusion of multi-headed flowers, with a colour range of cream, apricot, orange and shades of pink. Blooming in June for several weeks, they add excellent colour in the border, and are rewarding as a cut flower since they last so well in water.

Arranging. I think these flowers look very well in a vase on their own, perhaps with a little green foliage, but not enough to distract from their delicate colours; the greenish feathery heads of *Alchemilla mollis* make a good foil. Otherwise they can be used in groups of apricots or pinks. One or two stems tucked into the centre of an arrangement give added colour for the focal point, and as they can be cut short or left with long stems, they can be used in this way for almost any size of arrangement.

Conditioning and preserving. A long drink in deep water immediately after picking is really all that is necessary.

The seeds heads are attractive if allowed to form on the plant and then picked and hung upside down to dry. They can then be used full length for larger dried arrangements, or separate florets cut off for smaller arrangements.

Cultivation. Always buy pot-grown plants, and plant very carefully without damaging the roots. March or April are the best months to plant. Choose a sheltered spot, preferably against a south- or west-facing wall; and good garden soil is suitable. In all but the mildest areas protect the plants in winter with a 6 in (15 cm) layer of bracken, peat or straw. Pick sparingly for the first year or two. Some support with pea sticks may be necessary. Cut the stems down to the ground after flowering.

Anaphalis

Anaphalis margaritacea, height 12–18 in (30–45 cm), planting distance 12–15 in (30–40 cm); *A. nubigena*, height 8–12 in (20–30 cm), planting distance 12 in (30 cm).

These are useful plants with pleasant silvery foliage, providing a restful area in the border, particularly the dwarf *A. nubigena*.

Arranging. I find I use these flower heads mostly as dried material, in dried pictures, small arrangements and swags. However, they are nice for the centre of a green arrangement, but are good only if used with short stems. I cut them about 2 or 3 in (5–7.5 cm) long, and tuck them into the middle of a group as a focal point.

Conditioning and preserving. As I have indicated, the flower heads only last well in water if the stems are cut rather short. Condition by removing most of the foliage, then dip the stem ends into a little boiling water followed by a long drink.

For drying, bunch the flower heads on stems of about 5 in (13 cm), picking before the flowers have started to fluff, though they must be well open on the plant.

Cultivation. Plant from October to April in any good well-drained garden soil, in sun or shade. Good plants for dry conditions. *A. margaritacea* may need some support with twiggy sticks. Cut the stems down to the ground after flowering.

Anemone hybrida

(*A. japonica, A. elegans*), height 2–3 ft (60–90 cm), planting distance 12–18 in (30–45 cm).

Japanese anemones are particularly useful because they flower in early autumn. 'September Charm' and 'White Giant', both growing to 3 or 4 ft (around 1 m), produce clear pink or white single flowers that last well when cut.

Arranging. Enchanting on their own, these anemones can also be used effectively with green to make a green and white arrangement, or the pink-flowered varieties with grey leaves to produce a charming pink and grey vase.

Conditioning and preserving. The flowers last well without any special treatment.

Individual flower heads can be dried excellently using silica gel.

Cultivation. Plant from October to March in any well-drained good garden soil, preferably in partial shade, although these anemones will grow in sun. They like a moist soil and often take several years to flower well. Cut the stems down to the ground after flowering.

Angelica archangelica

Height 6–10 ft (2–3 m), spread 3 ft (1 m).

This plant is only suitable for a large garden, as it takes up lots of room and seeds so freely that it can become a real menace, though I love the big seed heads and fading pale green leaves. It will grow up to 6 ft (1·8 m) high, and needs staking in rough weather, so you can see it has limited value. The rounded seed heads can span a foot, but are usually about 9 in (23 cm) across. In spite of all its disadvantages, angelica is excellent for filling in space in a new garden.

Arranging. As the heads are so big, they are only useful for large arrangements, such as church groups, when they make a good focal point in a mixed green vase. However, the umbels of flower can be pulled apart and used in small arrangements.

Conditioning and preserving. All the stems, whether of flower or foliage, need the boiling water treatment: put the ends of the stems into 1 in (2·5 cm) of boiling water while you count up to ten, and then leave in deep cold water for as long as possible. Fill hollow stems with water and plug with Oasis.

To dry, leave the flower heads on the plant until the seed has formed, then cut and hang upside down.

Cultivation. Angelica is often grown as a biennial, but will live for several years if the flowers are removed. If plants are obtainable these may be planted in March in ordinary soil, preferably in a moist situation in sun or partial shade. Or seed may be sown in March or April in a prepared seed bed in the open. Transplant the seedlings 12 in (30 cm) apart when large enough, and move them to their final quarters in March of the following year.

Artemisia

Artemisia absinthium 'Lambrook Silver', height and spread 3 ft (1 m); *A. lactiflora*, height 3–5 ft (1–1·5 m), planting distance 18 in (45 cm).

Grey foliage plants, which look well in the border

and are useful for picking all through the summer months. *A. absinthium* is a small shrub. The only artemisia grown for flower is *A. lactiflora*, which has elegant cream plumes of flower.

Arranging. The flower plumes are a great standby for background in any arrangement from July onwards, using the stems at almost any length.

Conditioning and preserving. The plumes last longer if the stem ends are dipped into boiling water and then left in deep water for an hour or two. The plumes of 'Lambrook Silver' dry well in an arrangement in water, or if picked once the stem is in a mature state, and hung upside down to dry.

Cultivation. Plant from October to April in any good well-drained garden soil, in full sun for preference. *A. lactiflora* may be grown in partial shade, and the stems should be cut down to the ground after flowering. *A. absinthium* should be pruned in April each year, cutting the stems to about 6–8 in (15–20 cm) above ground.

Arum italicum 'Pictum'

Height 18 in (45 cm), planting distance 12 in (30 cm).

This is one of the greatest treasures in any garden. The small spade-shaped spotted leaves come straight out of the ground in December or early

Arum italicum

January, resisting the stormy weather by closing up and unfurling as the sun shines. They grow on short stems of about 3–4 in (7·5–10 cm), but the leaves get much larger as the months go by, and in May the stems are often 6 or 7 in (15–18 cm) long and the big leaves up to 12 in (30 cm) or more in length, though their size does depend on the soil conditions. Producing seed heads of thick clusters of iridescent red berries in the autumn, they are very decorative in the garden—but the birds also enjoy them, and the stems become pulpy and soft if they are put in a vase.

Arranging. The small leaves are such a good shape that they fit into any arrangement of foliage or of small spring flowers.

Conditioning. It is best to submerge the leaves completely overnight, or in a weak solution of starch.

Cultivation. Plant from September to December in any good garden soil, fairly moist, if possible in full sun.

Astrantia major
Height 2 ft (60 cm), planting distance 15 in (40 cm).

A shade-loving plant that seeds freely, its wiry stems holding delicate flower heads each a cluster of greenish-white or pinky florets within a collar of white bracts.

Arranging. These strange little flowers of nondescript appearance mix well in any small summer group. Though they grow on stems up to 12 in (30 cm) in height, I generally use them on shorter stems and tuck them well into the centre of a collection of small flowers.

Conditioning and preserving. The flowers last well in water with no special treatment.

I always think astrantia flowers should dry well, but in fact they don't. However, they can be preserved in a glycerine and water solution, turning a creamy-buff and keeping a perfect shape, making them ideal for use in swags and garlands of dried flowers as well as in small dried arrangements.

Cultivation. Plant from October to March in any good garden soil, in partial shade for preference, and in a damp corner if possible. Give the

support of twiggy sticks as the flower stems require it. Cut the stems down to ground level in the autumn.

Ballota pseudo-dictamnus
Height 18–24 in (45–60 cm), spread 2 ft (60 cm).

The arching shrubby growth of ballota produces graceful stems for flower arranging, though you have to remove nearly all the leaves as they completely cover the small clusters of grey-green flower bracts that circle the stems.

Arranging. As the flowers grow all down the stems, you really need to cut them as long as possible, or you will destroy the grace of the flowers. I find them most effective in an arrangement of mixed flowers, adding a touch of delicate green more unusual than foliage.

Conditioning and preserving. Place the ends of the stems into 1 in (2·5 cm) of boiling water for a count of twenty, then stand in deep cold water for an hour or two.

Ballota bracts will dry quite well and keep a good green colour if the leaves are removed and the stems, with well-opened flowers, are bunched and hung upside down.

Cultivation. Plant in spring—March, April— in any good garden soil, in full sun, but choose a well-drained spot that does not lie wet in winter. Prune in April, shortening the growths by about half their length.

Bergenia
Bergenia purpurascens 'Ballawley', height 12–15 in (30–40 cm), planting distance 2 ft (60 cm); *B. cordifolia*, height and planting distance 12 in (30 cm); *B. crassifolia*, height and planting distance 12 in (30 cm).

Without any doubt, bergenia is one of my favourite plant families: the rounded or heart-shaped fleshy leaves, useful in both summer and winter, make them a 'must' for every garden. They grow well in shade or full sun and act as excellent ground cover. *B. crassifolia* has spoon-shaped leaves that turn a bronze colour in winter, and has masses of delicate pink flowers in spring

Bergenia cordifolia

which are particularly welcome because they provide solid contrast to the more spiky spring bulbs. *B. cordifolia* has heart-shaped leaves that often turn beautiful autumnal colours as they die off. The newer hybrid 'Ballawley' has a leaf shape which is a cross between the two mentioned above, and turns a lovely deep bronze in winter.
Arranging. There is hardly a week in the year when I don't use some of these leaves. They are superb to add weight to the base of a foliage group, clustered in threes they add under-shadow to the arrangement, and will give a restful zone to a slightly cluttered arrangement of mixed flowers. The autumn-coloured leaves are marvellous with reds, or shades of apricot, in autumn. The magenta-pink flowers of *B. cordifolia* go well with reds in spring.
Conditioning. The leaves benefit from a good soak for a few hours in cold water. They are often limp if picked during a hard frost, but will soon recover if submerged in tepid water—and this means of course that they can be used however cold the weather.

Cultivation. Plant from October to March in any ordinary soil, including limy soils, in sun or partial shade. Cut off faded flower stems. Lift and divide plants every few years if they become overcrowded.

Campanula

Campanula carpatica, height 5–10 in (13–25 cm), planting distance 12–15 in (30–40 cm); *C. glomerata*, height up to 18 in (45 cm), planting distance 18–24 in (45–60 cm); *C. lactiflora*, height 3–5 ft (1–1·5 m), planting distance 18 in (45 cm); *C. latifolia*, height 4–5 ft (1–1·5 m), planting distance 18 in (45 cm); *C. persicifolia*, height 2–3 ft (60–90 cm), planting distance 12–18 in (30–45 cm); *C. portenschlagiana*, height 6 in (15 cm), planting distance 18–24 in (45–60 cm).

One of the best-lasting summer flowers, and a great asset for the flower arranger because the flowers continue to open in water from bud stage, and though paler and not so large as the first blooms, they do not drop their petals, which is a real joy after the lupin and delphinium period. *C. carpatica* is suitable for the rock garden, has lovely open flowers in clear white or blue. *C. portenschlagiana* makes a good edging plant and produces a mass of long-lasting purple bell

Campanula persicifolia

flowers, but is not good as a cut flower. *C. persicifolia* is the best for cutting and is now a popular plant in the cut flower trade. My grandmother grew these and had a wonderful collection of seedlings, with cup and saucer form, in white and blue. I wish I had valued them then as I do today! *C. glomerata* has many forms, but the varieties that bloom in May and June are the most useful, as they bring that early touch of colour to the garden, and are excellent solid heads to pick, though they do not last as well as some other campanulas when cut. One of my favourites is *C. latifolia*, especially the white form 'Alba' and the blue-flowered 'Gloaming'—but again these do not last well when cut. *C. lactiflora* 'Loddon Anna', pale pink and 'Prichard's Variety', violet-blue, are well worth having in any garden. They last well in the border and when cut.

Arranging. *C. persicifolia* must be my first choice in this family as the variety that lasts best when cut. The white forms mix well with greens and in a vase of all white summer flowers. The blue-flowered forms are splendid in mixed arrangements. I love to use *C. latifolia* in a semi-oriental arrangement because it has such a beautiful form and stands out so well in a simple white shallow dish, maybe just three stems on a pinholder and a few hosta leaves at the base. 'Loddon Anna', or any of the tall and stately heads of the *C. lactiflora* species, make a marvellous background for a large group for a church decoration or summer wedding.

Conditioning. *C. latifolia*, *C. glomerata* and *C. lactiflora* all need to have their stem ends burnt, by placing them in about 1 in (2.5 cm) of boiling water, counting twenty, filling the can up to the top with cold water and leaving the stems to drink for several hours. As a child, I remember the ritual of hammering the stems and then standing them in a bucket of water in the cellar for two days: they seemed to last for ever afterwards. The only treatment needed to make *C. persicifolia* last well is a long drink of cold deep water for a few hours.

Cultivation. Plant from October to March in any normal garden soil, in sun or partial shade. The taller varieties may need the support of twiggy sticks. Remove flower spikes when the flowers have faded, and cut down the old stems of the tall campanulas in the autumn.

Chrysanthemum

Chrysanthemum Korean varieties, height 2 ft (60 cm), planting distance 18 in (45 cm); *C. maximum* 'Esther Read', height 2 ft (60 cm), planting distance 12–18 in (30–45 cm).

From this large family of perennial flowers that are perhaps more widely grown than almost any other I have chosen only two varieties. The summer-flowering *C. maximum* 'Esther Read' which has a lovely double white flower, excellent for cutting and showy in the garden, deserves a place in every border. I cannot bear to see these lovely pure white flowers dyed every conceivable colour and sold all through the summer, but I think I must be alone in this as they are obviously very popular. 'Esther Read' grows to about 2 ft (60 cm), but there are many taller varieties of the Shasta Daisy.

My second choice is the autumn-flowering Korean chrysanthemums, not really hardy perhaps, though with a good top-dressing of leafmould my plants have withstood many winters. There is a wide range of colours, but my favourites are the single apricots and 'Wedding Day', a beautiful white with a green centre.

Arranging. 'Esther Read' chrysanthemums give good flower heads for arranging as they last so well in water with no dropping of petals, and I have known them keep for two weeks in the house if they are picked really fresh. They make a good show just on their own with no unrelated foliage, but they can of course be used with other white flowers. They make a marvellous focal point in any vase as they have outstandingly clear faces. Korean chrysanthemums also look lovely on their own—perhaps massed in a basket—or used for a central point in any vase of mixed flowers, or autumn-coloured foliage.

Conditioning. Bruise or hammer the ends of the stems and leave in a bucket of cold water up to their necks for three hours or more.

Cultivation. Plant 'Esther Read' from October to April in any good garden soil, in full sun or

Opposite
1 Tulip
2 Apple blossom
3 Iceland poppy
4 *Acer pseudoplatanus* 'Brilliantissimum'

The apricot colours of this arrangement blend well with their container—an alabaster *tazza*. The young, pale-pink shoots of *Acer* 'Brilliantissimum' are a subtle foil to the orange tulips and Shirley poppies.

Overleaf
1 Salix
2 *Helleborus foetidus*
3 *Helleborus orientalis* hybrid
4 Petasites
5 *Arum italicum*

This arrangement demonstrates the effectiveness of a plain white bowl to set off a group of green flowers and foliage.

partial shade. Cut down the old stems to the ground in the autumn.

Plant Korean chrysanthemums in April or May in any good garden soil, in sun or partial shade. Feed with a soluble fertilizer as directed by the makers, during the summer. Cut the old stems to the ground after flowering, and protect the plants with a 6 in (15 cm) layer of peat, straw or bracken.

Cimicifuga racemosa BLACK SNAKE-ROOT

Height 5–6 ft (around 1·7 m), planting distance 2 ft (60 cm).

Tall spikes of fluffy white flowers on coal-black stems, appearing in July and August, when there is very little tall material to cut and arrange.

Arranging. Stems of cimicifuga bring touches of delicacy to a vase of mixed flowers, and are

graceful in a shallow dish arrangement on a pin-holder with their own leaves at the base.

Conditioning. I find that the flowers last a little better if the ends of the stems are placed in boiling water for a few seconds before giving them a long drink of cold water.

Cultivation. Plant from October to April in any good garden soil, preferably in light shade in a site that is fairly moist. Support the flower stems with twiggy sticks if necessary, and cut the stems down to the ground after flowering.

Clematis

Clematis × *eriostemon*, height 3 ft (1 m), planting distance 2 ft (60 cm); *C. integrifolia*, height 2 ft (60 cm), planting distance 12 in (30 cm).

These unusual herbaceous plants deserve a place

78

in the garden for the added interest they bring. I have had *C. integrifolia* for more years than I care to mention, and it blooms continuously from June to September. It has deep purple-blue flowers with turned back petals, whereas *C.* × *eriostemon* grows in more bushy form, and the flowers are faintly perfumed.

Arranging. These unusual flowers add interest to a small mixed vase in high summer, providing the touch of blue which is so helpful to any mixed arrangement—I believe that blue and yellow are essential colours for any mixed vase. Though in some cases the flower stems can grow up to 3 ft (90 cm), I never cut them more than 5–6 in

(13–15 cm) long, as the charm is in the tiny flower. They therefore look best in small vases, being completely lost if used on long stems in a large arrangement.

Conditioning and preserving. The flowers last well if given a long drink of water before arranging.

The fluffy seed heads are most attractive for winter groups, but it is advisable to spray them with a little hair lacquer to prevent the seeds from disintegrating.

Cultivation. Plant herbaceous clematis from October to April in any good garden soil, preferably alkaline. They like a sunny aspect, and may need support of twiggy sticks.

Opposite
1 *Artemisia lactiflora*
2 Gladiolus
3 Nicotiana
4 Petunia
5 Stock
6 Hydrangea
7 Rose

A refreshing combination of creams and whites. It is important to keep the water clear when using a glass container and to hide the mechanics of the arrangement.

Page 81
Deep-pink camellias arranged in a pinholder on a simple pewter dish. These flowers always look best with their own dark glossy foliage.

Convallaria majalis LILY OF THE VALLEY
Height 8 in (20 cm), planting distance 4–6 in (10–15 cm).

Sweetly scented sprays of white bells, a most popular flower which has a strange habit of deciding for itself where it would like to grow. However carefully you plant it, it has a habit of spreading on to a nearby path, but try planting it there and in no way is it happy! However, it is well worth a spot in any garden; it likes shade and any soil, making it a good plant for the small town garden and excellent ground cover anywhere as few weeds can penetrate the dense green foliage.

Arranging. Because of their delicious scent, lilies of the valley are a joy to have in the house. They scarcely need arranging: just pick small bunches, surrounded by their own leaves, tie with string and pop into any pretty china bowl, sugar dish or sauce boat.

Conditioning. If picked straight from the garden, then an hour or two in deep warm water is all that is necessary. If bought out of season, then it is advisable to place the bunch, still wrapped, into deep warm water overnight, for it has usually been forced and will be very tender.

Cultivation. Plant in September or October in any good garden soil, preferably in a moist and shaded site. If it is possible to redirect rain from the down pipe of a roof gutter into the bed, this will often encourage the plants to grow strongly.

Crocosmia masonorum
Height 2½ ft (75 cm), planting distance 12 in (30 cm).

A valuable late-flowering summer plant with erect sword-like leaves from which slender flower stems of 2–3 ft (60–90 cm) arch out with their vivid orange clustered flowers. The foliage is as useful for the flower arranger as the flower. Once considered not to be hardy, it became very obscure, but is now widely grown with little trouble.

Arranging. The leaves are superb and make a wonderful background to a later summer green group, which really needs good spikes as much as rounded flowers or leaves. The flower heads with their clear orange colour are good outline material for such heavier autumn flowers as dahlias and chrysanthemums.

Conditioning and preserving. The flowers need little save a good long drink, as they last well in water.

The leaves can be preserved by putting the stem ends into a solution of glycerine, when they turn a lovely brown colour. They can also be pressed by putting the sprays between newspaper or blotting paper and placing them under a heavy book or carpet. Flower seed heads dry well on the plant and can be used for winter arrangements.

Cultivation. Plant in March or April in well-drained soil in a site sheltered from east and north winds. They need no support. Cut the withered stems and foliage down in March. In cold districts either lift and dry off the corms in October, keeping them free from frost, or cover them with a 6 in (15 cm) layer of peat, straw, bracken or half-decayed leaves.

Cynara
Cynara scolymus (globe artichoke), *C. cardunculus* (cardoon), height 4–5 ft (1–1.5 m), planting distance 2 ft (60 cm).

Globe artichokes and cardoons are useful for flower arranging and worth a place in any garden, though they take up quite a lot of space. Both plants have good grey foliage and tall stems producing big globe heads which open into thistle-like flowers. If you do not want to eat the artichokes, they are nevertheless very attractive in all stages, good to cut and striking when dried.

Arranging. There are so many ways of using these plants: the leaves are excellent for foliage arrangements, as a background with greys, or with any summer flowers. It is best to cut the flower heads with short stems, as they are so heavy that they can topple over the whole arrangement quite easily. When in the green stage they make a good focal point, and later in the summer the purple thistle-like heads can be used in big groups, maybe cutting the stems to not more than 8 in (20 cm). I also use the dried heads, either purple or brown, as a central point in the same way, and therefore on very short stems.

Conditioning and preserving. The flowers last very well in water with no additional help, but like all flowers they benefit from a really long drink before arrangement. The leaves do better if the ends of the stems are dipped into boiling water before they are given a long drink. Avoid submerging, for like most grey foliage the leaves have a covering of minute hairs, and if these get really wet for any length of time it tends to destroy the colour.

The flower heads dry well in full flower: leave them on the plant until they go a lovely brown colour, then pick them and hang upside down until thoroughly dry. They can be used like this, but are also attractive if the outside bracts are removed, leaving the centre of pale fawn-coloured fluff. It is advisable to spray the backs of the flowers with spray glue or cheap, sticky hair lacquer.

Cultivation. Plant in March or April in good soil enriched with compost or manure, in a well-drained, sunny site. Feed with a general fertilizer when new growth begins. Cut the stems and leaves down to 12 in (30 cm) above ground in late October, and earth them up as one would potatoes, but do not cover the stems. Lay bracken or straw in a layer of about 12 in (30 cm) thick up to but not over the stems. In periods of very severe frost cover the plants right over, but remove the covering when the weather turns mild again.

Each spring, in April, scrape the soil away and

reduce the number of shoots on each plant to three. This will encourage the production of strong flower stems and large heads. Make a new planting with some of the offsets that are removed. After the plants have given three crops, destroy them. Young plants will have been coming along to take their place. Plants older than three years become less prolific.

Delphinium

Belladonna varieties, 'Blue Bees' and 'Peace', height 3–4 ft (around 1 m), planting distance 2 ft (60 cm); Pacific hybrids, height 6–7 ft (around 2 m), planting distance 2–3 ft (60–90 cm).

Delphinium blue is so often talked about that it comes as quite a shock when you see lovely spikes of white delphiniums and some of the most subtle shades of pink and purple. The Pacific hybrids grow on tall stems, so they are naturally subjects for the back of the border; though the smaller Belladonna types are becoming more and more popular as they need little staking, yet give the blue which is needed both for garden and flower arranging.

Arranging. Delphiniums have a wide range of uses: nothing is prettier than a vase full of them on their own if you can spare enough. The white varieties are superb for any mixed white arrangement, and with philadelphus and white peonies for instance, make the perfect wedding arrangement. A stem of purplish pink with pink roses emphasizes the pink, or with pale mauve picks out that colour. Blues and lime greens are another excellent colour scheme, and delphiniums make these arrangements easy. The small Belladonna varieties are so well worth growing, and they are marvellous to arrange; the stems are only about 3 ft (90 cm), and they can be used full length or on short stems, and strangely enough do not look out of proportion—though I would hate to cut down the long stems of giant delphiniums. So the large blooms of the Pacific hybrids need large containers, to show off the grace and elegance of these flowers. It is comforting to know that if they are too well grown and too big they are not so useful for the flower arranger.

Conditioning and preserving. The art of keeping delphiniums in water is mostly a question of being careful to pick them before all the flowers are open right up the stem, leaving some buds at the top. The buds will not open in water, but at this stage the lower flowers are not too far open and will last several days without dropping. I find that as they start to drop it is best to shake every bloom each morning, instead of leaving the petals to fall all the time and make such a mess. The tip of filling the hollow stem with water and plugging with oasis or cotton wool can help, and I find that the old idea of adding a little starch to the water does seem to help prevent the petals dropping.

Delphiniums hold their colour well when dried if the stems are hung upside down: use the smaller stems or side shoots when the blooms are well open right up the stem. Single florets or small stems dry well in silica gel, or some similar drying powder, but when these are taken out of the powder and used in the house, they must always be kept in a very dry atmosphere. The green seed heads dry well if picked just as they have formed and hung upside down.

Cultivation. Plant from October to March in any good garden soil enriched by digging in compost or manure. A sheltered but sunny site is desirable. Tall varieties need staking with four bamboo canes and string tied across from cane to cane to form a kind of network to support the flower spikes. The Belladonna varieties need only twiggy pea sticks to keep them upright.

After flowering cut spikes to just above a strong leaf. New flowering shoots may appear to bloom in the late summer. In October or November cut the plants down to ground level.

Dianthus   PINKS

Height up to 18 in (45 cm), planting distance 8–12 in (20–30 cm).

Pinks conjure up for me hot summer days from my childhood: in my memory there seem to have been so many of them, and I always associate them with the scent of pinks edging the borders. The beds in the vegetable garden, too, were always edged with 'Mrs Sinkins'—no pink in my opinion is more fragrant. The grey tussocks of foliage and wealth of small pink, red or white flowers make pinks ideal plants for the front of the border or for the rock garden.

Arranging. As with so many sweet-scented flowers, pinks need little arranging, and can be picked into your hand in a bunch and popped into a small vase or pretty piece of decorative china: a little flower-painted cup is ideal. The stems are short and they can be used in any small summer arrangement, their tiny rounded faces making a good focal point in any small group.

Conditioning and preserving. No special conditioning is required, for they last well in water; but never leave them out of water before arranging, for if they once fade they will never recover.

The small seed heads are useful for drying and using in miniatures or small winter dried arrangements.

Cultivation. Plant from October to March, or even later if the plants are pot grown as they usually are. They prefer a sunny open site, well drained. They do not object to some lime in the soil, but a limy soil is not essential. Some support with twiggy sticks is necessary for the taller pinks. Do not mulch pinks with organic material as this may cause the stems to rot. Feed after flowering with a good general fertilizer.

Dicentra spectabilis

Height 18–24 in (45–60 cm), planting distance 18 in (45 cm).

'Bleeding Heart' as it is often called, is a plant of great charm with decorative foliage and arching sprays of flowers that hang like small hearts when in bud, and appear very early, making it doubly useful as a cut flower as it is well ahead of many other herbaceous plants. It is low-growing and a welcome subject for the front of the border. If you take one of the flowers, turn it upside down and pull back the petals, you will reveal what looks like a lady in her bath—a little trick that gave us a lot of fun when we were children.

Arranging. Stems with a natural curve are heaven-sent for the flower arranger, and dicentra is effective as outline material for any small arrangement, whether of a mixed group with tulips and other bulbs, or of a vase on its own with no unrelated foliage.

Conditioning and preserving. Dip the ends of the stems into boiling water until you count ten—it needs very little time as the stems are fleshy and boiling water creeps up them very quickly—then allow an hour or so in deep cold water.

Small sprays can be preserved in silica gel, giving good arching shapes that can be used in little flower pictures, but they do not stand well enough without support for use in dried arrangements.

Cultivation. Plant from October to March in

Dicentra spectabilis

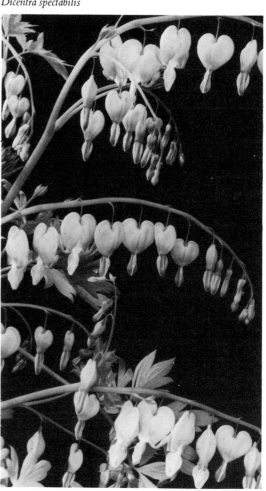

any good garden soil; work in compost or manure before planting. Dicentras thrive in full sun, but do not object to some shade. As they flower so early they do need protection from cold winds, and are best planted in a south-west or west-facing position, where the sun will not reach them too early on frosty mornings.

Dictamnus albus

(*D. fraxinella*), height 2 ft (60 cm), planting distance 18 in (45 cm).

This is known as the 'Burning Bush' and, if you hold a lighted match to the base of the flower stem on the evening of a hot day, it will ignite and burn off oil without harming the bush. I long to try this but have never dared. The flowers are rather similar to a lupin at first glance, but with long stamens in white and mauve-pink.

Arranging. The flower spikes are pretty, very unusual and last well in water, making them ideal for use in all-white or green and white arrangements. There is a purple form (*D. albus* 'Purpureus') which enhances any mixture of interesting material.

Conditioning and preserving. The flower spikes should be given a long drink in warm water.

The good seed heads dry well if cut and hung upside down.

Cultivation. Plant from October to March in a sunny, open, well-drained site. Any reasonably good soil is suitable, preferably alkaline. Acid soils may be given a dressing of lime at the rate of 4 oz to the square yard. Cut the plant down to ground level in the autumn. No staking is required.

Digitalis

D. grandiflora (*D. ambigua*), height 2–3 ft (60–90 cm); *D. parviflora*, height 3 ft (90 cm), planting distance 18 in (45 cm); *D. purpurea* 'Sutton's Apricot', height up to 5 ft (1·5 m), planting distance 2 ft (60 cm).

The biennial foxglove, 'Sutton's Apricot', is superb, particularly in woodland as it thrives in partial shade. The tall spikes of apricot last well in water. Among the perennials, *D. grandiflora* has dark green foliage and pale yellow bells, while *D. parviflora* has flowers of mauve-pink and buff.

Arranging. *D. parviflora* has such unusual colouring that I find it goes well with many colour combinations, and it has a short stocky growth habit that is most useful. The taller foxgloves produce stems of up to 5 ft (1·5 m), making them ideal for the large wedding group or any church arrangement, and the soft colouring of the Sutton's variety enables one to use it with all kinds of yellow and apricot groups. Do be careful to pick with stems as long as possible, as these flowers lose all their elegance if arranged on too-short stems.

Conditioning and preserving. Put the ends of the stems into warm water and allow them to have a long drink.

To dry, pick stems when the seed heads have formed, remove all the foliage and hang upside down until dry.

Cultivation. Plant from October to March in any good garden soil, in sun or, preferably, light shade, in a moist spot if possible. They will flourish, however, in dry shade if well watered when necessary.

Seeds may be sown in May in a prepared seed bed outdoors. Transplant the seedlings 6 in (15 cm) apart when large enough, and transfer to their permanent positions in autumn or spring.

Cut away the main spike when the flowers fade to encourage side growths, and in autumn cut the plant down to ground level.

Epimedium × rubrum

Height 12–15 in (30–40 cm), planting distance 12 in (30 cm).

Epimediums have become more popular in recent years, not only because of their interesting foliage for flower arrangers, but also as a ground cover plant. The leaves are wonderful to cut when they have matured on the plant. The flowers are adorable, coming before the leaves on wiry stems supporting delicate columbine-like sprays in white, pale or deeper pink. Sadly, they do not last well, though I have used them on special occasions; but it is the foliage that I use continuously through late summer and autumn, when the leaves turn wonderful bronzy colours.

Arranging. The autumn-coloured leaves look marvellous with sprays of berries, dark red dahlias, blackberries, and dark beetroot leaves; but they have many other uses because of their unusual form and striking colouring. The foliage is also superb in spring, and I often think that the creamy-apricot colour of the new leaf growth is as effecttive as the tiny sprays of flowers; however, it is not advisable to pick them, as at this stage of growth they cannot be made to last for more than a few hours in water.

Conditioning. It is essential at all times to dip the ends of the leaf stems into boiling water up to a count of twenty, and then let them have a long drink of cold deep water. The flowers need the same treatment. If you should decide to use the young spring foliage, try submerging it completely and leaving overnight in cold water.

Cultivation. Plant from October to March in partial shade in any reasonable soil. If there is danger of the plants drying out in summer, they will need watering in dry spells. No pruning is required.

Eryngium giganteum

Height 3–4 ft (around 1 m), planting distance 2 ft (60 cm).

A hardy biennial with grey-green foliage and flowers with a silvery collar of prickly spines surrounding a blue-grey head. They are most decorative both in the house and garden.

Arranging. These thistle-like heads add a lovely centre to a green group, and are particularly striking in an arrangement of greys and pinks. In fact, I find that they enhance any arrangement, and I can never get enough of them.

Conditioning and preserving. The fresh flower heads need little conditioning, but benefit from a long deep drink of cold water.

If the stems of the open 'flowers' are put into a glycerine solution, they take on a slightly oily appearance and never shed their bracts, so I can thoroughly recommend this. You can dry them

Eryngium giganteum

by hanging the heads upside down, but they do not stay open quite so well, so it really is worth the extra trouble of glycerining them as they are so beautiful and last for months.

Cultivation. This biennial species dies after flowering so seed should be sown each year in a pot or box of a proprietary seed sowing compost in March in a greenhouse or cold frame. The seedlings are pricked off singly into Jiffy pots or Jiffy 7's, and planted out from October to March. Or seeds may be sown in the open ground in April, and the seedlings transplanted in the autumn. Any good garden soil is suitable, and a sunny site is best.

Euphorbia

Euphorbia characias, height 3–4 ft (around 1 m), planting distance 3 ft (90 cm); *E. griffithii* 'Fireglow', height 2½ ft (75 cm), planting distance 2 ft (60 cm); *E. myrsinites*, height 6 in (15 cm), planting distance 12 in (30 cm); *E. polychroma* (*E. epithymoides*), height 18 in (45 cm), planting distance 2 ft (60 cm); *E. robbiae*, height 18 in (45 cm), planting distance 2 ft (60 cm); *E. veneta* (*E. wulfenii*), height 3–4 ft (around 1 m), planting distance 4 ft (1·2 m). Not hardy: *E. fulgens*, height 4 ft (1·2 m), spread 12–18 in (30–45 cm); *E. pulcherrima*, height 4–5 ft (1–1·5 m), spread 1–2 ft (30–60 cm).

Euphorbia characias

The hardy euphorbias are numerous, and it is difficult to make the choice of which species to grow. Most make bushy plants that can be used in shrub or herbaceous borders and are rewarding for their colour and for the length of their flowering period. As far as I am concerned, they are another 'must' both for house and garden. *E. veneta* (*E. wulfenii*) is the most handsome of all, with good foliage all the year round and, in Graham Thomas's words, 'evergreen bottlebrushes on long stems, composed of dark grey-green leaves, forming heads 6 in (15 cm) wide. These leafy shoots are biennial and in their second year bear a big head of greeny-yellow small flowers'. These cut superbly, but if left on the plant will last several months. Though the foliage of *E. characias* is similar, the flower heads are not so handsome, being darker green with a black eye. *E. polychroma* has stems of about 18 in (45 cm) and is a subject for the front of the border, a joy in early spring with massed heads of sulphur-

yellow which are most effective. *E. griffithii* 'Fireglow' should be placed farther back, as it will grow up higher. It flowers a little later, in June, and the flower tips are brilliant burnt orange. *E. myrsinites* is more suitable for a rock garden or wall, flourishes on poor soil with lots of sun, and in those conditions produces good silver-green foliage which is attractive all the year, and heads of lime-yellow flowers in spring. *E. robbiae* is better in the odd corner and acts as a marvellous ground cover, with decorative dark-green tufted foliage, from which comes the yellowish-green flower spike.

If you live in a tropical area, then you will grow and love two other euphorbias: *E. fulgens*, which has arching sprays of tiny orange flowers clustered down the stems, and lasts very well indeed in water; and *E. pulcherrima*, the poinsettia that we know so well as a Christmas houseplant, which in its natural state grows to a bush 5 or 6 ft (around 1·7 m) tall and produces an abundance of flowers with red or pink bracts that last for months.

Arranging. The distinctive lime-green colour of euphorbia flowers looks well in any arrangement or in the centre of an all-green group. I use the foliage of *E. veneta* during the winter, and the flower heads from May to July: they fade as they mature, but are a vivid yellow-green in early spring. *E. robbiae* has a long flowering period and the particular asset of being useful in autumn, when the flower heads turn orange and are good with dahlias, gladioli and other bright autumn flowers.

Conditioning. All euphorbias ooze a white sticky juice, which is exceedingly poisonous and for some a nasty skin irritant. It is therefore very important to wash this off hands and secateurs, and to get the stems into water as soon as possible. I dip the ends into boiling water, counting up to twenty and then allow at least twelve hours in deep cool water. The more water they take up at this stage, the longer they will last. The ends of the stems can be singed in a gas flame with equally good results, but they must still be given a really long drink.

Cultivation. Plant from September to April in good well-drained soil, preferably in a sunny site. *E. robbiae*, however, enjoys shade, but may need watering in dry spells. Trim flowering stems in autumn to keep the plants shapely.

Opposite
 1 Prunella
 2 Gladiolus
 3 Alstroemeria
 4 Dahlia
 5 Hypericum berries
 6 Iceland poppy
 7 Tellima
 8 *Cobaea scandens*
 9 Beetroot leaf
10 Alchemilla

Overleaf
 1 *Euphorbia robbiae*
 2 Phlox
 3 Teazle
 4 Sedum
 5 Hosta
 6 Pelargonium
 7 Lime

An elegant gold cupid vase highlights the apricot tones of a few, mixed summer flowers. Lime-green alchemillas blend in well with most colours.

Mixed greens and yellows with their cool and refreshing tones can give pleasure at all times of the year. The beauty of a green arrangement is that it lasts so well and has no petals to shed. It is perhaps for this reason that it is one of the most satisfactory arrangements anyone can do.

Filipendula ulmaria 'Aurea'

Height 18 in (45 cm), planting distance 12 in (30 cm).

This is the only filipendula which I personally feel is suitable for this book. In spring it is one of the most attractive foliage plants, with brilliant golden divided and veined leaves, both in basal clumps and right up the flower stem. As the plant flowers, the leaves lose some of their vivid colour, fading to a creamy yellow. The flowers are insignificant, and I usually cut them off to retain the beauty of the foliage a little longer. My plant grows on heavy soil, and I find that it spreads and seeds well.

Arranging. The well-shaped golden leaves are useful in a green arrangement or at the base of a group of small yellow flowers. I find that the leaves last better as they mature on the plant, but even then they are a little hard to condition, so I use them only where I can look after them as I describe below. I occasionally use the flowers to add a light touch to a small mixed vase.

Conditioning. The small leaves should have their ends dipped into 1 in (2·5 cm) of boiling water for a few seconds and then totally submerged under cold water for several hours. In this way you give them every chance to drink. If you pick and condition some each day, you can replace any that have wilted; but if this is not possible, remove

Page 93
1 Delphinium
2 Poppy
3 Rose
4 Marigold
5 Dianthus
6 Stock
7 *Clematis integrifolia* (herbaceous)
8 Alchemilla
9 Euphorbia
10 Amaranthus

A display of mixed summer flowers. It is important in such an arrangement to include blue and yellow but to avoid white as it is too prominent.

Opposite
1 *Euphorbia wulfenii*
2 *Senecio clivorum* 'Desdemona'
3 Arum
4 *Valeriana phu*
  and hellebores

This olive-green pottery water jug makes a suitable container for this unusual green and yellow arrangement. Here I have tried to follow the lines of the fish through with the tallest stem of euphorbia. The arrangement is outlined with a collection of my favourite flowers—hellebores, valeriana, senecio and arum foliage. Green arrangements, such as this one, are simple to do but effective.

any wilted leaves from the vase and submerge them again, overnight if possible.

Cultivation. Plant from October to March in partial shade in a moist spot if possible. The plant is not fussy about soil. Cut the stems down to the ground in autumn.

Gentiana

Gentiana acaulis, height 3 in (7·5 cm), planting distance 12 in (30 cm); *G. asclepiadea* (willow gentian), height 18–24 in (45–60 cm), planting distance 12–18 in (30–45 cm); *G. sino-ornata*, height 6 in (15 cm), planting distance 12 in (30 cm).

The willow gentian brings a lovely patch of blue to the garden in late July, and the flowers are so graceful in an arrangement. Growing on slender stems, the trumpet-shaped blue flowers are borne in the leaf axils down the stem. *G. sino-ornata* has vivid blue flowers on short stems, and if it grows well produces a sheet of blue in September. It loves the conditions in Scotland and I have never seen it growing better than there. *G. acaulis* has larger flowers of an even deeper blue and firm green leaves, flourishes on lime soils and flowers in the spring.

Arranging. The small gentians, *G. acaulis* and *G. sino-ornata*, add that important touch of blue to any small arrangement, and it is therefore desirable to have both as they flower at different times of year. A miniature white china vase filled with blue gentians looks really marvellous, but remember to place them in a good light as they tend to lose their colour in artificial light. I have only recently got my clump of willow gentian well enough established to be able to pick and enjoy these lovely arching sprays. Arranged with mauve asters, the last sprays of catmint and some pink roses, they add a sharp colour and a graceful outline.

Conditioning and preserving. The small gentians need little conditioning, but I do dip the stem ends of the tall gentian in a little boiling water and then allow a long drink.

G. *acaulis* and G. *sino-ornata* flowers preserve well in silica gel. I find that the willow gentian dries well in water and keeps a good colour all winter if you remove all the leaves and keep the stems in a vase of water in a warm place. They will also quite often dry off if they are simply left in the vase in which you have arranged them.

Cultivation. Plant *G. asclepiadea* and *G. acaulis* from September to March, in full sun, in reasonably fertile soil enriched with peat or garden compost. Plant *G. sino-ornata* in March or April in a sunny position; lime-free soil is essential. Work in peat or well-decayed leaf-mould at planting time.

Geranium CRANES-BILL

Geranium × 'Johnson's Blue', height 12 in (30 cm), planting distance 2 ft (60 cm); *G. sanguineum*, height 12 in (30 cm), planting distance 18 in (45 cm).

All true geraniums are hardy, and are not to be confused with the indoor and summer bedding 'geraniums' which are pelargoniums. The cranesbills have a wide range of colours and heights, and though they are not good for cutting, I cannot pass *G. sanguineum* without recommending it. I have grown it for so many years and it has given me endless weeks of pleasure, with its large leafy

Geranium × 'Johnson's Blue'

clumps and brilliant magenta flowers, blooming for weeks and needing little attention. G. × 'Johnson's Blue' I think is the best blue geranium, and both these plants will adapt to the odd corner and give small good-coloured flowers to pick in high summer.

Arranging. If the magenta flowers of *G. sanguineum* are picked on short stems, they can be used to give a touch of brilliant colour to a small posy of mixed summer flowers. 'Johnson's Blue' short-stemmed blue-mauve flowers are a pretty addition to the blue and mauve arrangements that are only possible at this time of year.

Conditioning. The flowers last longer if cut on short stems and given a long drink in warm water. The autumn-tinted leaves are tempting to pick and will survive well enough for 24 hours, but there is little chance of their lasting longer.

Cultivation. Plant from October to March in sun or partial shade. Any reasonably fertile soil is suitable provided it does not lie wet in winter. Cut the flower stems to the ground after flowering, and cut the plant down to ground level in the autumn. The plants may need some support with twiggy sticks.

Grasses

Briza maxima, height 18 in (45 cm), planting distance 8–12 in (20–30 cm); *Cortaderia selloana* (*C. argentea*), height 6–8 ft (around 2 m), planting distance 4–6 ft (1–2 m); *Elymus arenaria*, height 4 ft (1·2 m), planting distance 12 in (30 cm); *Lagurus ovatus*, height 12 in (30 cm), planting distance 6 in (15 cm).

Perennial grasses bring wonderful variations of colour and form to the shrub border with their clumps of feathery flowers and spiky foliage in many shades of green. In the same way they add variety and a light touch to summer arrangements and dried groups.

C. selloana, or pampas grass, is a majestic plant when in full flower, and can look well in grass or as a foreground to evergreen shrubs. *E. arenaria*, like silver wheat, has good grey foliage even before flowering, and though it needs careful watching if it is not to take over the whole border, it is not difficult to control.

Arranging. The thin flowering stems in a glass goblet or wine glass look so effective placed either in front of a window or behind a light. I also love to use an arrangement of dried leaves and seed heads in the house in winter, and dried grasses really make the arrangement. Pick when the flowers are fully open.

Conditioning and preserving. Give all grasses a long drink of water as soon as they have been picked.

When they are in flower or in seed, the grasses will take up glycerine well. The nodding heads of *B. maxima* and *L. ovatus* are particularly well worth doing as they look rather shiny, don't shed and last for weeks. For glycerining, remember again to pick only when the flowers are really open.

Pampas and elymus dry well if left in 1 in (2·5 cm) of water in a warm room.

Cultivation. Plant cortaderia and elymus from September to March. These grasses grow in any reasonable soil and prefer an open sunny site. Cut them down to ground level in October or November. *B. maxima* and *L. ovatus*, however, are annuals and may be sown in March or April in the open ground where they are to remain in their flowering position.

Helleborus

Helleborus foetidus, height 2 ft (60 cm), planting distance 18–24 in (45–60 cm); *H. lividus* sub-species *corsicus*, height and planting distance 2 ft (60 cm); *H. niger*, height 12–18 in (30–45 cm), planting distance 18 in (45 cm); *H. orientalis*, height 18–24 in (45–60 cm), planting distance 2 ft (60 cm).

Another necessity for both garden and flower arranger. *H. niger*, the Christmas Rose, has pure white wide-open nodding flowers held erect, with a cluster of bright yellow stamens in the centre of each bloom. *H. orientalis* hybrids (the Lenten roses), produce longer flower stems and a lovely range of colours from greenish-white or pink and purple tinged to an almost black plum colour, their nodding heads giving a wonderful show in spring. The green variety that most of us still think of as *H. corsicus* (but which at the moment is called *H. lividus ssp. corsicus*) has the most beautiful foliage, each leaf made up of three prickly edged grey-green leaflets, lasting well when cut. The flowers are open green clustered heads of a mass of flowers standing on stems of about 18 in (45 cm). Some of my plants must be at least 20 years old, and seem to have had little attention but a top dressing of well-rotted manure in spring. *H. foetidus* has green bell-shaped pendent flowers and well cut, deeply divided dark-green foliage.

Arranging. The Christmas Rose can be forced under a pane of glass to ensure that the flowers are really out by Christmas, for nothing makes a more beautiful Christmas Day table decoration than a bowl of variegated holly, yellow jasmine and *H. niger*. They are a real joy, too, arranged with *Iris unguicularis*, winter jasmine, sweet-scented sarcococca or *Chimonanthus fragrans*. The *H. orientalis* hybrids are difficult to condition to make them last any length of time, but they are beautiful arranged in a shallow bowl so that the stems are well under the water. I have a small ornamental Italian vase in the shape of a lamb which holds flowers in its back, and for some reason the *H. orientalis* hybrids last extremely well in it, maybe just because the stems are in deep water.

All the green-flowered hellebores are wonderful to arrange, the lovely heads lasting very well indeed, and I pick them from January to June, using small florets in an early spring moss garden, and the full-length stems for the next few months.

Conditioning and preserving. All hellebores last better if their stem ends are hammered or dipped into 1 in (2·5 cm) of boiling water for several minutes, and then allowed to stand in deep water for twelve hours or more. I find that by pricking the stems in several places, from just under the head to the base of the stem, they last pretty well once they have had a long drink. The orientalis hybrids flag after a few days, and then it is important to submerge them in cold water overnight; this can be repeated several times. A lot of trouble perhaps, but well worth it from my point of view, when flowers at this time of year are scarce and precious.

The seed heads of *H. niger* and some *H. orientalis* hybrids dry well if they are picked after the seed heads have formed on the plants, the stems placed in a little water and left in a warm place.

The flowers of *H. lividus ssp. corsicus* dry well in silica gel, if you are careful to choose widely open florets.

Cultivation. Plant from October to March in any reasonably fertile soil, in partial shade. If a moist spot can be found that does not lie too wet in winter, so much the better. The only attention required beyond mulching with compost or mushroom manure in April, is to cut down withered leaves or stems from time to time.

Hemerocallis   DAY LILY

Hybrids, height 2–3 ft (60–90 cm), planting distance 18 in (45 cm).

This plant is to be recommended as much for its early spring foliage of brilliant green as for its flowers. Day lilies are widely grown in America, with flowers in really beautiful colourings, making the common orange-yellow dull by comparison. They need little attention—mine have been in the

Hemerocallis (mixed)

garden for more years than I like to think about, and seem to thrive on neglect—but grown with a bit more care, some of these new hybrids make a fine display. The flowers really do last for only one day, but the buds continue to come out all the time, even in water.

Arranging. I use the early foliage a great deal as it is graceful and iris-like, providing a sharp touch of emerald green in a foliage arrangement or in a vase of spring flowers. Although I enjoy the flowers I cannot really recommend them for the focal point of an arrangement, since each flower lasts only for the day, and you may well find that you have to wait for a couple of days without your vital centre until the next flower comes out. However, the buff and brownish colouring of some day lilies is so lovely that it is worth using them somewhere, even if the effect is short-lived. The florets look effective floating in a shallow bowl.

Conditioning. The early spring foliage lasts better if the stem ends are dipped into boiling water and then given a long drink for several hours; as the summer goes on, this treatment is no longer necessary. The flower stems need no special treatment, though as always they benefit from a long drink of warm water before arranging.

Cultivation. Plant in any reasonably fertile soil from October to March, in sun or partial shade. Water well in very dry spells. Tidy the plants up in autumn, cutting them back to within 1–2 in (2·5–5 cm) of the ground.

Heuchera

Bressingham hybrids: 'Bridget Bloom', 'Greenfinch', 'Scintillation', height 18–24 in (45–60 cm), planting distance 12 in (30 cm).

The evergreen ivy-shaped marbled leaves make this a marvellous plant for ground cover and for flower arranging, with foliage that is copper in spring and bronze in winter. The delicate stems of small bell-shaped flowers range from pale-pink to scarlet in the Bressingham hybrids. 'Greenfinch' is outstanding for the flower arranger, with real green flower spikes.

Arranging. The delicate flower stems add a graceful touch to a vase of small summer flowers in pretty coral shades. I use the leaves all the year round: they make a restful placement at the base of miniature arrangements, some having excellent markings and lovely bronzy colours.

Conditioning. The flower stems last well if allowed just a long drink in warm water. The leaves should be submerged overnight, or at least for a few hours.

Cultivation. Plant between October and April preferably in light quick-draining soil, in sun or partial shade. The plants tend to lift themselves out of the soil, so they appreciate a mulch of compost, peat or mushroom manure.

Hosta

Hosta albo-marginata, height and planting distance 18 in (45 cm); *H. crispula*, height and planting distance 2 ft (60 cm); *H. fortunei* 'Albo-picta', height 18–24 in (45–60 cm), planting distance 18 in (45 cm); *H. sieboldiana*, height and planting distance 2 ft (60 cm); *H. × 'Thomas Hogg'*, height 2 ft (60 cm), planting distance 18 in (45 cm).

With the wide range of these wonderful leaf plants, it is really difficult to pick out the best, and I think you must be guided by the amount of

Hosta fortunei 'Aurea'

space you can allow for them. They produce large clumps of superb foliage, the size of leaf depending on the growing conditions: if in good damp soil and half-shade, the leaves are enormous and some get as big as 20 in (50 cm) in length, but the average size is about 12 in (30 cm). Having so many forms and colours of green, they are decorative in the garden from May to October, or until the first frosts, and they are also wonderful to use in arrangements, making the hosta a 'must' for everyone, however small the area that you are working on. *H. albo-marginata* has one of the smaller leaves—about 9 in (23 cm)—sage green edged with a white band. *H.* × 'Thomas Hogg' has a white edge on a large leaf, as does the rarer *H. crispula*. *H. fortunei* 'Albo-picta' is perhaps my favourite, especially in spring when the leaves unfurl and display their lovely bright butter-yellow leaves edged with pale green—a remarkable sight. The yellow colour gradually fades and by midsummer the whole leaf is green. *H. sieboldiana* 'Elegans' is the greyest of all. The leaves can grow to 8 in (20 cm) in width, on stems of at least 2–3 ft (60–90 cm), making them extremely useful for picking. The flowers are sturdier than most hostas and a paler lilac colour. The smallest hosta that I use for flower arranging is *H. undulata*, with slightly contorted leaves, rich green and striped with central bands of white which vary on every leaf, and good deep-purple flower spikes on stems 18 in (45 cm) high. I also have a hosta with large greyish leaves edged in gold which I think must be *H. fortunei* 'Aureomarginata'. It appears to be rather rare, but is well worth searching for. Some of the smaller species of hosta from Japan are collectors' plants, but have little value for the flower arranger.

Arranging. There is scarcely a day all through the summer when I do not use a leaf of hosta. In early May, the leaves of *H. fortunei* 'Albo-picta' make the undershadow for a vase of near-blacks and lime greens using Delavayi peonies and dark auriculas. Hosta leaves are also excellent to use in any green group, as you can see from the illustrations. The tall and elegant flower stems, with their lilac pendulous bells, are good in any mixed flower group, especially with mauves and pinks.

Conditioning and preserving. An added joy about this plant is that the leaves stand so well in water. When they are in their early stages of growth I dip the stem ends into 1 in (2·5 cm) of boiling water and then submerge the leaves completely under cold water overnight. Then I place them in a polythene bag for several days, which stiffens them. But by the end of May little treatment is necessary, other than a long deep drink for several hours, or if possible overnight. The flowers last well with no special care.

To preserve the seed heads it is best to leave them on the plant till well formed and starting to dry, but be sure to pick before they have opened. Place them in a jug with a little water in a warm place and you can watch with delight as the heads burst open to reveal the jet-black clustered seeds. Unexpectedly they stay like this all winter.

The leaves can be pressed in autumn in the usual way between blotting paper or newspaper. In Canada they are placed between sheets of grease-proof paper and pressed with a warm iron and then allowed to dry off completely for another 24 hours under a heavy weight. By this means they keep their colour extremely well, though sometimes, if they are a little limp, it is necessary to place a piece of florist's wire at their backs and tape it on. They can then be placed at the base of a dried flower arrangement, providing a good solid leaf of natural colour.

Cultivation. Plant from October to March, in sun or, for the variegated forms, preferably in partial shade. Any reasonably fertile soil is suitable, but it is wise to dig in plenty of peat, compost or mushroom manure. Choose if possible a moist site, or arrange to water generously in dry spells if the soil tends to dry out. Tidy the plants up in autumn and, if material is available, give them a mulch in April.

Iris

Bearded iris, height 2–5 ft (60 cm–1·5 m), planting distance 18 in (45 cm); *Iris foetidissima*, height and planting distance 18 in (45 cm); *I. histrioides*, height and planting distance 4 in (10 cm); *I. pallida* 'Argenteo-variegata', height 3 ft (90 cm), planting distance 18 in (45 cm); *I. pseudacorus* 'Variegata', height 3–4 ft (around 1 m), planting distance 2–3 ft (60–90 cm); *I. reticulata*, height 6 in (15 cm), planting distance 4 in (10 cm); *I. sibirica*, height 2–3 ft (60–90 cm), planting distance 2 ft (60 cm); *I. unguicularis* (*I. stylosa*), height 12 in (30 cm), planting distance 18 in (45 cm).

The flag or bearded iris blooms in May, growing out of clumps of decorative blade-shaped grey-green foliage, in itself decorative all the year. The colour range of these flowers is fantastic, and often the upper and lower petals are of completely different shades, though I prefer the self-coloured types for arranging, such as: 'White City' and 'Magic Hills', good grey-whites; 'Canary Bird' and 'Golden Planet', clear yellows; 'Prairie Sunset', a beautiful pinky-apricot blend of unusual colouring; 'Tuscan', a copper brown; and two unusual blues, 'Blue Admiral' and 'My Smoky'. These are rather off-beat colours which are good for arranging, but there are endless other varieties from which to choose.

I. pseudacorus 'Variegata' is worth a place in any garden, with handsome yellow and green striped foliage in the early spring. *I. pallida* 'Argenteo-variegata' has shorter white and green striped leaves. *I. foetidissima* has good dark-green shiny

Iris sibirica

foliage, but I grow it for the seed pods, which burst in autumn displaying bright orange berries that stay in the pods nearly all winter if picked and kept indoors. The flowers of *I. sibirica* are in various shades of blue, and last well when cut.

A very desirable plant for the base of a south-facing wall is *I. unguicularis* (*I. stylosa*) which flowers from November to March, producing masses of fragile, scented purple flowers on short stems. Finally, two very early irises especially suitable for the rock or sink garden: *I. histrioides*, pale china blue with short sturdy stems, but producing a sheet of blue once established; and *I. reticulata*, in all the purple and blue shades, which grow a little taller and last well when cut.

Arranging. I find that the most interesting arrangements are started off by the use of one unusual-coloured flower which catches my eye, and then I go round the garden to see what would blend, or maybe contrast with it. Some of the tall bearded irises have this effect, and I find them ideal in groups based on Dutch flower paintings. Their foliage, too, is useful in large arrangements all the year round. *I. unguicularis* flowers are a joy, appearing so early in the year, though they should be picked in bud so that one can have the delight of watching the delicate purple blooms unfurl. They do not last longer than two or three days, but can be replaced quite easily, and in an arrangement with Christmas roses, winter jasmine, the first crocus and winter aconites, make a vase to cheer any winter's day.

Because of their short stems, *I. histrioides* may last better if arranged in a bed of moss, putting a layer of moss over wire netting, so that the early primroses and crocus, snowdrops and these iris all get added moisture, however short their stems may be.

The seed heads of *I. foetidissima* make a good central point in an autumn arrangement, the bright orange berries going well with pieces of autumn-coloured foliage. The leaves of *I. pseudacorus* 'Variegata', buttercup yellow in early spring, bring an effect of sunlight to any arrangement, and are especially helpful in a vase of mixed foliage.

Conditioning and preserving. No special

treatment is needed, though they should be given a long drink before arranging. Remember to remove each flower as it fades, for it will soon be replaced by a new one as the buds open in water.

To preserve the seed pods of *I. foetidissima*, I think it best to stand the stems in a little water and allow them to dry off in a warm room.

Cultivation. Plant the bulbous irises *I. histrioides* and *I. reticulata* from September to the end of November in full sun in light quick-draining but fertile soil. They need no attention beyond removal of the dead foliage in June.

Plant bearded irises and *I. pallida* in June or July, or in September, in any reasonably fertile soil, in full sun. *I. pseudacorus* may be planted in March, April or in September and October. It will grow happily in up to 18 in (45 cm) of water, but when grown in a border will be much shorter. Plant *I. foetidissima* in a moist border for preference in October or November, *I. sibirica* in preferably moist conditions, in September, October or April. *I. unguicularis* may be planted in September or April, preferably in a border at the foot of a south-facing wall. All these irises thrive in an open situation in reasonably fertile ordinary garden soil.

Kniphofia   RED–HOT POKER

'Brimstone', 'Bee's Sunset', 'Earliest of All', 'Jenny Bloom', 'Maid of Orleans', height 3–3½ ft (around 1 m), planting distance 2 ft (60 cm).

Kniphofias range in size from 6 ft (1·8 m) down to 18 in (45 cm), and come in so many different forms that the blooming period covers several months, from June to October. All have flame-like flowers on thick stiff stems. My favourites are the unusual creamy white 'Maid of Orleans'; the pure deep yellow 'Brimstone', which is late flowering; 'Earliest of All', the first of the flame-coloured forms and a good apricot-red; and 'Bee's Sunset' which I have heard described as a glowing orange. All these have gone a long way to improve the original form, *K. uvaria*, but the original plant still gives a wonderful display in the late summer and autumn garden.

Arranging. There are few flowers that have tall orange or apricot-coloured spikes, and for this reason and because they last well when cut, I find red-hot pokers most helpful from June to October. They add the vital tall slim background material for so many apricot and orange arrangements, with full-blown apricot roses, late dahlias and turning autumn foliage. They can be used on stems of their full height of 3 or 4 ft (around 1m) or cut shorter, but to avoid losing the grace of the plant I would advise against cutting a stem of less than 6 in (15 cm) below the flower head. These shorter pieces can be used at any angle, at the sides of an arrangement as well as in the centre where greater height is needed.

Conditioning. They last extremely well in water with no more care than a really long deep drink after picking. So far I have found no way of preserving them.

Opposite
1 Honesty
2 Phytolacca
3 Parsley
4 Rose

Dark pods of honesty and phytolacca are a perfect foil to 'Pink Chiffon' roses in this bronze container.

Cultivation. Plant from October to March in full sun, in any reasonably fertile soil. Tie the leaves together wigwam fashion in October to protect the crown of the plant from frost. 'Maid of Orleans' is not so hardy as other varieties, and in really severe spells may need a 6 in (15 cm) covering of straw or bracken. Trim the old foliage away in the spring.

Lupinus   LUPIN

Lupinus arboreus, height 3–4 ft (around 1 m), planting distance 3 ft (90 cm); *L. polyphyllus* varieties, height 3–4 ft (around 1 m), planting distance 2 ft (60 cm).

Thanks to Mr George Russell, who spent his life hybridizing the familiar herbaceous lupin, we have a wonderful strain of these decorative plants with colours ranging from pink to deepest red and white, through yellows to apricot shades.

The tree lupin, *L. arboreus*, bears a mass of sweetly scented yellow flowers in mid-June and these last for 2 or 3 weeks.

Opposite
1 Honesty
2 Agapanthus
3 Hydrangea
4 Rose

A blend of mauves and pinks—ideal for high summer. Hydrangeas need careful treatment to last well.

Arranging. With their fantastic colour range, lupins play a very important part in any of my flower arrangements in early June. I use the apricot shades with some apricot foxgloves and, some early apricot roses, such as 'School Girl', in a copper container; white lupins in an all-white or green and white group; purple lupins with other blue and mauve flowers; pink lupins in a pink and grey arrangement, and so on. A small basket filled with tree lupins in a mass is heavenly and the scent penetrates every room in the house.

Conditioning and preserving. There are many theories about how best to keep lupins. I find that filling the hollow stems with water does help. Standing the stems in a weak starch solution will prevent them from shedding petals everywhere, and this water can be added to the water in which they are arranged. If left in a vase of water or starch water overnight before they are arranged, you will find that they take on strange curves which you can use in your arrangement, for they will not change back again.

Only the seed heads are worth preserving. Allow these to form on the plant, then pick the stems, remove all their leaves, tie in bunches and hang upside down to dry. You will have to use your discretion about doing this, since the good hybrids are best not allowed to set seed.

Cultivation. Plant from October to March in full sun or partial shade, in any good garden soil, even in limy soils. Cut flower stems when flowers have faded, and cut the stems down to the ground in the autumn. Normally they do not require any support, but on rich soil in exposed positions a few pea sticks may be needed.

Macleaya

Macleaya cordata 'Coral Plume', height 5–8 ft (1·5–2 m), planting distance 3 ft (1 m).

Growing up to 7 ft (2 m) or more in height and inclined to spread (though easily checked) this is a subject for the back of the border, with plumes of pinkish-buff coloured starry flowers, feathery in appearance. The large rounded lobed leaves are grey-backed or grey-green turning buff and golden, and the plant looks particularly effective placed in clumps among shrubs.

Arranging. The coral flower plumes are a wonderful background for any apricot, buff or beige-toned arrangements, and I use the superb leaves frequently in large arrangements.

Conditioning and preserving. Do not cut the flowers until they are fully open to the top of the stem. Then dip the stem ends in boiling water for a count of twenty, followed by a drink in deep cold water overnight. Individual leaves should be treated in the same way.

The flower stems form a lovely tracery effect once they shed their petals, and in this form they are well worth keeping for use as background material in dried or winter arrangements.

Cultivation. Plant from October to March in any fertile soil, in full sun but sheltered from prevailing winds. In exposed gardens some support of pea sticks may be needed. Cut stems down to the ground in the autumn.

Nepeta

Nepeta × faassenii (*N. mussinii*), height 18 in (45 cm), planting distance 12 in (30 cm).

Known as catmint—and cats really do love it—this makes an excellent ground cover with very aromatic grey foliage and spires of mauve flowers. It flowers almost non-stop from June to October, but is at its best in July.

Arranging. I first saw these flowers used in an arrangement many years ago, when they were placed round the edge of a shallow bowl and the centre filled with roses. I still think they look pretty used like this, but find now that they also make a good background for a small urn-type vase of mauve and blue flowers, and look particularly lovely with 'New Dawn' roses.

Conditioning. All these flowers need is a long drink in deep warm water as soon as they have been picked.

Cultivation. Plant from October to April in full sun or partial shade, in any reasonably good garden soil. Cut the plants down to the ground in November.

Onopordum salteri

Height 10 ft (3 m), planting distance 3 ft (1 m).

A most handsome grey thistle, towering up to the sky, of statuesque beauty with prickly grey leaves and purple Scottish-thistle like flowers—though I really much prefer the plant before these open. It needs quite a lot of space as it grows up to 10 ft (3 m), but makes the most wonderful silhouette against an evening sky or dark trees.

Arranging. When fully grown, the large leaves make a wonderful base for a really big group. The small side shoots add good grey colour and lovely form to smaller arrangements. Just before the flowers break colour, I use a long stem of the grey buds and foliage with other greys, or as a background for blues or mixed greens.

Conditioning and preserving. Foliage stems and individual leaves all last better if the ends are dipped into boiling water until you count twenty, and are then given a deep drink in cold water overnight.

When the flowers are well open, they can be picked and hung up to dry, and sometimes retain a good purple colour.

Cultivation. A biennial which may be sown in the open ground in spring in any good garden soil.

Osmunda regalis

Height 4–5 ft (1–1·5 m), planting distance 4 ft (1·2 m).

Worthy of its name, the Royal Fern, this is the largest and most handsome hardy fern. The fronds are copper-brown when they first unfurl, turning green as they lose their early pale-brown woolly covering, and taking on beautiful yellow-brown tints in autumn.

Arranging. Avoid the temptation of picking in spring, for the fronds will not last well in water unless they are mature on the plant. Once they are green, you will need a vase large enough to take the handsome stems, and then you will find they make good background material, especially for an all-green arrangement. If used in autumn, there is the possibility that they may curl, so I find it better to used pressed leaves with autumn colourings, when again they make a marvellous outline.

Conditioning and preserving. Dip the ends of the stems into boiling water and leave for several minutes, and then submerge the whole leaf in a bath of cold water for as long as possible.

To preserve, take the fronds when either green or of good autumn colour, and press between sheets of newspaper under a carpet for several days. When dry the stems often need support, and I find it is best to place a really long piece of wire against the back of the stem and then twist fine wire round both at about three points up the stem.

Cultivation. Plant from October to March in sun or partial shade, in reasonably fertile soil—the richer the better. Work in compost or peat, and give a mulch in April. Cut the old stems down to the base in autumn.

Pachysandra terminalis

Height 12 in (30 cm), planting distance 18 in (45 cm).

Undoubtedly one of the best ground-cover plants. *P. procumbens*, which is native to America, is widely grown in that country, yet rarely seen in Britain. The dark-green close-growing serrated leaves of *P. terminalis* make a wonderful carpet beneath trees and shrubs. There is a variegated form which is also effective, though less rapid in growth.

Arranging. The leaves of pachysandra will last for weeks in water, so much so that they will grow roots. They are very pleasing arranged alone; and make a good base or fill-in for spring flowers, and for this purpose the variegated form is especially good as it is lighter in appearance.

Conditioning and preserving. Give a deep drink in cold water for several hours.

Individual leaves press well for use in flower pictures. As the stems last for literally months in water, they need no additional preserving.

Cultivation. Plant in early autumn or March in any reasonably fertile soil that is moisture retentive but not liable to be waterlogged, preferably in partial or total shade. It does best in lime-free soil.

Paeonia lutea ludlowii × delavayi 'Ann Ross'

Paeonia   PEONY

Shrub peonies: *Paeonia delavayi* and hybrids, height and spread 6 ft (2 m); *P. lutea ludlowii* and hybrids, height and spread 4–6 ft (1–2 m); *P. suffruticosa* hybrids, height and spread 5–6 ft (1·5–2 m).
Herbaceous peonies: *P. lactiflora* hybrids, height 2 ft (60 cm), planting distance 2½–3 ft (75–90 cm).

Choosing peonies is as difficult as choosing roses, for so much depends on your personal taste. I prefer the soft colours, and these with white would always be my first choice, but I also use some of the brilliant colours in mixed arrangements.

Shrub peonies grow to about 5 ft (1·5 m), and bear single blooms usually smaller in flower than those of the herbaceous varieties. *P. delavayi* has maroon single small flowers, but I have some Sarson hybrids with larger and beautiful flowers. *P. lutea ludlowii* has sweetly scented single yellow flowers, also rather small, and good seed heads. Hybrids of the tree peony, *P. suffruticosa*, are a 'must' for the garden, and given shelter from the wind they are lovely plants to grow. 'Hakugan' and 'Mrs William Kelway' both have superb single white flowers and lovely foliage which turns yellowy-bronze in autumn. 'Souvenir de la Reine

Elizabeth' has enormous double pink flowers spanning 9–12 in (23–30 cm). 'Lord Selbourne' has flowers of a soft blush-pink with similar large heads opening in June. The red-tinted buds appearing from March onwards, and the good leaf colour make this an interesting plant all the year round. The *P. lutea* hybrid 'Souvenir de Maxime Cornu' bears huge pale-yellow flowers tinged with red that tend to hang their very heavy heads, and are better with support for their full beauty.

The herbaceous peonies, hybrids of *P. lactiflora*, are among the very best plants for the garden and can be grown in clumps among shrubs. 'Sarah Bernhardt' is still one of the most outstanding peonies of all time, with double sugar-pink heads flowering in July—rather later than the average time for this group—and producing an abundance of blooms once established. 'Solange' is one of my favourites, amber on creamy buff large heads of which I can never get enough. 'Kelway's Queen' blush-white tinted coral, is another outstanding peony. 'Duchesse de Nemours', sulphur-white incurved, and 'White Wings' are I think the best white singles. Others I would recommend are 'Beau Geste', semi-double flowers in brilliant glowing carmine; 'Lord Kitchener', single blooms of intense maroon-red; 'Dresden', a blush-white single; and 'Pink Delight', a good pink. If you are fortunate enough to be able to get some of the Sanders' hybrid peonies from North America, try the superb 'Janis', with a lovely apricot-coloured single flower appearing in May. Sylvia Sanders hybridized peonies for the greater part of her life.

Arranging. Peonies are for me the highlight of the summer, making a spectacular centre for any group, whether it is in all-white, white and pinks, scarlets or an arrangement in pastel shades. Two single shrub peonies and a stem of walnut with its red-brown furry bark make a most pleasing arrangement. Both single and double blooms are beautiful: I used to be very fond of the double flowers but now feel that I almost prefer singles. As they can withstand intense cold and hot summers, they grow marvellously in North America, and some of the best peonies I have ever used for arranging came in by ship from Canada

every summer before the war. Alas, one never sees them now.

Conditioning and preserving. If you can bring yourself to do it, peonies last better if cut and laid on a cool stone floor overnight: then cut off the stem ends and put them in warm water. They can be kept in a really cold freezer room for several weeks if necessary, but the buds must be showing colour before the stems are picked, and they should be placed in airtight plastic bags and left until required. Again, you should cut the ends of the stems when they are taken out of the bags, and put into warm water for several hours. Though you may lose one or two, it is well worth trying this method for some very special occasion.

The seed heads of the shrubs such as *P. delavayi* last well if picked when green, and hung upside down to dry. The open flowers of the herbaceous peonies can be dried in flower-drying powder, but the temperature must be very high to allow them to dry off really quickly. They keep their colour beautifully if dried at a temperature never lower than 65° F (15° C), which is not always easy in Britain, but I have seen the most lovely vases of them in America.

The leaves of tree peonies glycerine well, giving you an interesting leaf shape for a dried arrangement in winter. For glycerining, it is best to pick the leaves when they are still green.

Cultivation. Plant from October to March in any good garden soil enriched by digging in old manure or compost. Choose a sheltered site if possible, in full sun or partial shade.

Shrubby peony varieties are usually grafted on to a vigorous stock so the union where the graft was made should be buried 3–4 in (7·5–10 cm) below the surface to encourage rooting of the scion (the grafted variety). Conversely, the crowns of herbaceous peonies should not be covered more than 1 in (2·5 cm) deep with soil or they may fail to flower. It is important to remember this when applying mulches in subsequent years—do not cover the crown of the plant (where the growth buds are) more than 1 in (2·5 cm) deep. Mulch generously all peonies in April, give water in dry spells, and cut herbaceous peonies down to the ground in the autumn.

No pruning beyond cutting out dead wood is required on shrubby peonies.

Papaver · POPPY

Papaver nudicaule (biennial), height 1½–2½ ft (45–75 cm), planting distance 12–18 in (30–45 cm); *P. orientale* 'Perry's White', 'Mrs Perry' (perennials), height 2–3 ft (60–90 cm), planting distance 2 ft (60 cm); *P. rhoeas* (annual), height 2 ft (60 cm), planting distance 1 ft (30 cm); *P. somniferum* (annual), height 2½ ft (75 cm), planting distance 1 ft (30 cm).

Poppies not only provide so much colour in the garden, but can be cut and last surprisingly well in the house. The Orientals mentioned above, 'Perry's White' and 'Mrs Perry', the latter a soft pink, are to be recommended, as are the off-beat colours of the art shades, and though it is difficult to get seed of these, plants are still available. Shirley Poppies, *P. rhoeas*, come in a wide range of colours, white and pink-mauve to red, but though I do use them as cut flowers, I really grow them for their delightful seed heads, excellent for so

Papaver orientale

many dried arrangements. The Iceland poppy, *P. nudicaule*, is one of my favourites, delicate transparent-looking little flowers in colours ranging from white to apricot, salmon-pink and clear orange. This poppy is listed as a perennial, but I find is better grown as an annual. The big blowsy peony-flowered annual poppy, *P. somniferum*, in soft shades of pink, mauve, white and deep red, are easily grown and seed themselves freely, but I do scatter some ripe seeds each year where I hope they will grow.

Arranging. These are flowers that need careful preparation, and may be thought attractive by only a limited number of people; but if you are a keen arranger, then I think you will find the open-faced flowers of such a delightful colour range well worth the effort of growing and conditioning. I use the art shades in large arrangements, with Preston hybrid lilacs, pink cherry blossom and lupins, and they provide a wonderful focal point. The small Iceland poppies are beautiful if arranged with grasses, and in a delicate glass container, their hairy stems look pretty seen through the clear water.

Conditioning and preserving. All poppies should have their stem ends burnt, either in a gas flame or by putting them into 1 in (2·5 cm) of boiling water, and they should then be allowed a really long drink in cold water for several hours. I like to cut the stems at different lengths, to avoid re-boiling after cutting: it is essential to re-boil or burn if you do cut the stems shorter before arranging.

Poppy seed heads preserve well and are a great asset for garlands, dried hanging balls, etc. The Oriental, opium and small Shirley poppies all produce heads that can be used in these ways. Let the seed dry on the plant, giving them some protection against birds who will otherwise peck the seeds as soon as they are ripe. Cut the stems, strip off the foliage, and hang them upside down until the heads are thoroughly dry.

Cultivation. Plant *P. orientale* and its varieties from October to March in any normal garden soil. Give some support with twiggy sticks if necessary. Cut the stems down to the ground in the autumn.

Sow *P. nudicaule* in May or June in the flowering site, and thin to the planting distance indicated— or transplant to this distance very carefully.

Sow the annual poppies in March or April, and thin the seedlings to the planting distance as indicated.

Penstemon

Penstemon fruticosus 'Cardwellii', height and planting distance 1 ft (30 cm); *P. hartwegii* 'Garnet', height 2 ft (30 cm), planting distance 1 ft (30 cm); *P. laevigatus* 'Digitalis', height 3–4 ft (around 1 m), planting distance 1 ft (30 cm).

One of the problems with penstemons is that they are not truly hardy, but once they are established they flower continuously from June to September with spikes of bell-like flowers on stems of about 2 ft (60 cm). 'Garnet' is almost the hardiest, but the more striking blooms are those of *P. laevigatus* 'Digitalis', with flowers resembling a foxglove, as the name indicates. The blue *P. fruticosus* 'Cardwellii' is well worth growing, and provides that touch of blue so welcome for the flower arranger. It is advisable to take cuttings frequently, as it tends suddenly to die out.

Arranging. Penstemons are not entirely reliable as a cut flower, but they are so lovely in a mixed vase in summer that I take a chance, and replace any that wilt. They look superb used in a basket of summer flowers.

Conditioning. Conditioning is essential. Pick when the flower is well open, remove as much foliage as possible, dip the stem ends into 1 in (2·5 cm) of boiling water, and then allow at least a night in deep water, but the longer the better.

Cultivation. Plant in March or April in full sun in any reasonably fertile soil provided it does not lie wet in winter. Cut the stems down to ground level and protect from severe frosts with a cloche or even some bracken or straw.

Petasites

Petasites fragans, P. japonicus 'Giganteus', height 1 ft (30 cm), planting distance 4 ft (1·2 m).

A plant only to be grown by those of you who have a large piece of unwanted land and you really do not know what to do with it. It is definitely not suitable for a spare corner, or under trees, or indeed anywhere in a small garden. *P. fragrans* grows wild in many areas, and is a joy to pick for its strange little fragrant pink flowers. *P. japonicus* 'Giganteus' has bright green flower spikes appearing well before the frill of enormous leaves. These large leaves and the plant's tendency to spread rapidly are the great problems, but it is none the less a magnificent plant for the waterside.

Arranging. The cone-shaped green flower head is wonderful in mid-February or early March, providing a solid centre for any vase of mixed green, and looks enchanting with stems of green hellebore and catkins. And I find that arranged in a bowl on their own, these flowers of *P. japonicus* 'Giganteus' will make a talking point at any dinner party.

Conditioning. The flower heads stand well with little special treatment, but I advise you to pick them a few days before you intend to use them, as the stems are so short that they are difficult to use when cut. If you can leave them in a vase of water, you will be surprised to find how quickly they grow, making it much easier to use them effectively.

Cultivation. These plants need no cultivation. Plant from October to March in any waste land, and let the plant take it over. Do not, however, let it escape into any cultivated part of your property. It is a ground-cover plant *par excellence*.

Phlox

Phlox paniculata (*P. decussata*) hybrids: 'Admiral' 'Daily Sketch', 'Mother of Pearl', 'Sandringham', 'Vintage Wine', etc., height 2½–3 ft (75–90 cm), planting distance 18 in (45 cm).

The scent of phlox on a hot summer's day brings back so many memories. They form a patch of excellent colour from mid-July all through August, just when the garden is starting to become completely dependent on annuals, and are well worth growing on that account, in spite of being greedy feeders and lovers of moisture. I have chosen a few varieties for their colours: 'Admiral' is a very good white; 'Mother of Pearl' a soft pink; 'Sandringham' and 'Daily Sketch' both good pinks with a darker eye. There are many good reds, especially 'Vintage Wine' which suits its name perfectly, as does 'Star Fire'; and 'Prince of Orange' is an excellent orange. The mauves and lilacs are particularly good colours for mixed summer arrangements.

Arranging. A mass of mixed coloured phlox in a large wooden bowl will scent the room on a midsummer's day. Like all arrangements using only one type of flower, this takes a lot of material and you may feel as loath as I do to pick so much all at one time. But phlox look just as well in one-colour groups, and a few stems of white phlox can make an ideal centre for a mixed white vase in July.

Conditioning. Though phlox last well with little special treatment, they benefit from a long drink in deep warm water before arranging. This should be done straight after picking, because if they are allowed to flag the flower stems will not recover. Remove some of the foliage before arranging, and always check each day to remove any dead flower heads: if they are left they make the whole stem look tired, and as the buds continue to open in water, it is particularly important to remove all dead heads.

Cultivation. Plant from October to March in any ordinary garden soil, in full sun. Plant 6 in (15 cm) deep. Mulch every year with peat or compost in April as phlox roots tend to appear on the surface. They need plenty of water in dry spells. On established clumps reduce the shoots to about eight or ten in the spring. Cut off the top 2 or 3 in (5–7.5 cm) of some of these when they are about two-thirds of their final height, to encourage side growths that will flower later than the normal shoots. Cut the stems down to the ground in the autumn.

Phytolacca americana

VIRGINIAN POKE WEED

Height 4–8 ft (1–2.5 m), planting distance 3 ft (1 m).

A perennial plant standing from about 4 to 8 ft

Phytolacca americana

(1–2 m) high, with nondescript flowers, but excellent seed heads forming right up the stem, starting green and turning black by autumn.

Arranging. If you use the seed heads as soon as they form, the long green spikes of close green seeds can be cut to any length according to where you wish to place them in the vase, either for an outline or for the centre of the arrangement. As they turn black they are ideal for a black and white arrangement, or with autumn-coloured material and berries. Care must be taken to see that the overripe seeds do not fall, as they can stain badly: understandable, I suppose, for they were used as a dye many years ago. The seeds are also poisonous.

Conditioning and preserving. The flower stems of phytolacca should have their ends put into boiling water and then given a long drink. Seed heads need little extra care, but remove the foliage as this fades very quickly. The only reason for drying is to save the seed, which is the best way to propagate the plant.

Cultivation. Plant from October to April in sun or shade, in any good garden soil. In exposed gardens give the plants some support. Cut the stems down to ground level in the late autumn.

Polygonatum   SOLOMON'S SEAL

Polygonatum multiflorum (P. hybridum), height 2–4 ft (60 cm–1 m), planting distance 12–18 in (30–45 cm).

A hardy perennial with arching stems clothed in pairs of green leaves and white pendent bell flowers. It grows well in shade and is found growing in woods in its natural state. In garden cultivation, the stems grow to 2 or 4 ft (60 cm–1 m), or rather less in shady situations.

Arranging. Without doubt one of the most useful flowers to grow for flower arranging. I use the stems all summer: their graceful arching form is invaluable as outline and to give a natural curve to balance the base of a vase. When in the green stage, I find them perfect for an all-green group, and later, when they are turning gold in autumn, I feel they enhance almost any autumn arrangement.

Conditioning and preserving. No special treatment is required to make the stems last well in water. They take up glycerine very well and, though rather limp, retain a good golden brown colour.

Cultivation. Plant from October to March in any good well-drained garden soil. The plant enjoys full sun, but should be planted so that its roots are shaded. It also appreciates a suitable mulch in April. Cut the stems down to the ground in November.

Polygonum

Polygonum affine 'Donald Lowndes', height 9 in (23 cm), planting distance 18 in (45 cm); *P. aubertii*, height and spread 20 ft (6 m); *P. bistorta* 'Superbum', height 2½–3 ft (75–90 cm), planting distance 2 ft (60 cm); *P. cuspidatum* 'Variegatum', height 8 ft (2·5 m), planting distance 6 ft (2 m).

Another vast genus, but the ones I have listed here are well worth growing. *P. bistorta* 'Superbum', growing to about 3 ft (90 cm), sends up small poker spikes of deep pink in May, and continues intermittently till autumn. *P. affine* 'Donald Lowndes' has short 8 in (20 cm) stems of deep pink flowers, which appear on and off all summer, turning a deeper colour as the winter approaches. These low spreading varieties provide good

ground cover and are useful on a bank, especially since the foliage turns russet red in autumn. The tall shrub species, *P. cuspidatum*, should be mentioned, but it is a rapid spreader and therefore only useful in a spare corner. The variegated form, *P. cuspidatum* 'Variegatum' is not so rampant, and with good variegated leaves it mixes well in the shrub border. The pink-flowered climber *P. aubertii*, often confused with *P. baldschuanicum*, is widely grown in America, and dries well.

Arranging. Small pieces of *P. bistorta* 'Superbum' are good in mixed vases in May, and the odd stems that flower later are always useful. 'Donald Lowndes' can be used in small arrangements and their deeper shades later in the year are lovely in autumn-coloured arrangements.

Conditioning and preserving. For the shrub type and taller varieties, dip the stem ends in boiling water and follow with a long drink.

The deep pink stems of 'Donald Lowndes' preserve well if the heads are hung upside down. To dry *P. aubertii*, strip off the leaves after picking the stems, then place them in a vase with a little water, or hang them upside down.

Cultivation. Plant from October to March in good garden soil, in sun or partial shade; a moist situation is best. Trim flower stems to the base after flowering in the autumn. *P. aubertii* may be trimmed hard with shears in spring to keep it within bounds.

Primula

Primula auricula, height and planting distance 6 in (15 cm); *P. denticulata*, height and planting distance 12 in (30 cm); *P. rosea*, height and planting distance 6–8 in (15–20 cm); *P. vulgaris*, height and planting distance 6 in (15 cm).

A vast family, in which I have included just a few of my favourite species and also the hardy auricula and the polyanthus.

The wild primrose, *P. vulgaris*, with its open small yellow or sometimes pink flowers on short stems is good for woodland underplanting to make a lovely show in spring. *P. rosea* 'Delight' is a mass of bright pink flowers in early spring, suitable for rock garden or scree. We have to grow *P. malacoides* as a greenhouse plant, but I have seen this primula with flowers in all shades of pink and mauve growing in great drifts of colour in California, looking superb beneath camellias.

I grow the deliciously scented hardy auriculas for their wonderfully subtle colour range. They are sometimes known as Dusty Millers, for their white flour-dusted foliage. The Polyanthus needs no description, with its multi-headed primrose-like flower stem and excellent colour range of white, yellows, pinks, blue and orange.

Arranging. I use wild primroses in early spring, either in a little basket arranged on a bed of leaves, or individual bunches placed in a bed of moss. The rock species of primula, *P. rosea* or *P. denticulata*, with its rounded purple heads, mix well with small spring flowers, or in a moss garden. Polyanthus flowers can be used through the whole spring and summer, as they often bloom at strange times of year. A mass of polyanthuses in a wooden box looks so right and attractive, though stems of separate colours added to any spring vase are also an asset. *P. malacoides* flowers are rarely used as cut flowers, as they are too precious, but they look lovely in a planted dish garden.

Conditioning. Primroses, if picked wild in quantity, are better bunched and kept in a polythene bag until arranged. Polyanthus flowers last longer in arrangements if the stems are pricked with a pin just under the head and then allowed a long drink of water. Auriculas last well with no special treatment other than a long drink.

Cultivation. Plant from October to March. Any good garden soil is suitable, preferably one that is moisture retentive. *P. rosea* particularly revels in moist, even boggy conditions. They enjoy full sun, but also thrive in partial shade. Work in plenty of compost or other organic manure before planting; mulch generously in April and give plenty of water during dry spells.

Prunella grandiflora
Height 6–12 in (15–30 cm), planting distance 18 in (45 cm).

Deep purple flowers on 9–12 in (23–30 cm) stems, making a good carpet of colour for the front of the border, or under roses.

Arranging. The solid purple flower spikes come in useful as infilling material for a mixed blue and purple arrangement in June or July.

Conditioning and preserving. The flowers last well with no special treatment.

The seed heads preserve excellently, and this is one of my main reasons for growing the plant. The stems with seed heads can be hung upside down to dry, or allowed to dry in a vase with a little water.

Cultivation. Plant from October to March in any good garden soil, in sun or partial shade. On dry soils water in hot dry spells. Trim over flower stems as necessary.

Pulmonaria
Pulmonaria angustifolia 'Azurea', height and planting distance 12 in (30 cm); *P. saccharata* 'Pink Dawn', height and planting distance 12 in (30 cm).

Good for underplanting, for it flowers early and stays in bloom for nearly two months. The earliest is P. *angustifolia* 'Azurea' with flowers that are at first pink and then a brilliant blue, so that you often get a couple of pink bells amongst the gentian-blue ones. 'Pink Dawn' has flowers of pale mauve-pink and lovely foliage, particularly desirable because it lasts well all summer.

Arranging. The very early blooms make a lovely touch of colour in a moss garden, or in any small vase of spring flowers. The leaves of 'Pink Dawn' are effective but difficult to condition, though I use them in midsummer.

Conditioning. The small flower stems should be plunged into very deep warm water for several hours; the leaves require burning and overnight submerging. Take care to remove a small piece of the lower part of the leaf before arranging, as otherwise this may cause siphoning—water held by the hairs on the lower part of the leaf dripping over the side of the vase.

Cultivation. Plant in any reasonably good soil from October to March. While pulmonarias will grow in full sun, they need plenty of water in dry spells, and are really happier in partial shade, and they appreciate a good mulch of peat or similar material in April.

Pulsatilla vulgaris   PASQUE FLOWER
Height 12 in (30 cm), planting distance 15 in (40 cm).

The spring-flowering Pasque Flower is a beautiful plant with tufts of deeply cut leaves and nodding flowers in mauve, purple or white on short stems.
Arranging. Pulsatillas are a great asset in a vase of mixed small spring flowers.
Conditioning and preserving. The flowers last well without any particular treatment. They are followed by enchanting fluffy seed heads.
Cultivation. Plant from October to March in any well-drained reasonably fertile garden soil, in full sun.

Ranunculus
Ranunculus aconitifolius 'Flore-pleno', height 2 ft (60 cm), planting distance 12–18 in (30–45 cm); *R. asiaticus*, height 12 in (30 cm), planting distance 6 in (15 cm); *R. bulbosus* 'Pleniflorus' (*R. bulbosus* 'Speciosus Plenus'), height 12 in (30 cm), planting distance 18 in (45 cm).

R. bulbosus 'Pleniflorus' grows to about 18 in (45 cm) and has double yellow flowers, often with green centres. *R. aconitifolius* 'Flore-pleno' (Fair Maids of France) produces perfect double white button flowers for 3 months from May. Both these herbaceous varieties enjoy moisture. The tuberous rooted Persian and Turban varieties of *R. asiaticus*, thriving in the warmth of Florida, California and Kenya, are grown here as annuals—though never doing well for me—and are a popular cut flower. They have a wonderful range of colours in orange reds, white and pinks; both the single and double forms are good for the flower arranger.
Arranging. The herbaceous varieties are useful throughout the summer, particularly a few white stems for a white and green arrangement, or the yellows for a lovely splash of pure yellow in any arrangement of mixed yellows. The Turban ranunculus gives a focal point to any arrangement.
Conditioning. Herbaceous ranunculus lasts better

Ranunculus aconitifolius 'Flore-pleno'

if the stem ends are dipped into 1 in (2·5 cm) of boiling water and then given a long drink. For *R. asiaticus* varieties, the ends should be cut and the stems left in deep water for several hours. Whether you buy them or are lucky enough to grow them, they improve in every way after a night in deep water.
Cultivation. Plant *R. aconitifolius* and *R. bulbosus* from October to March, *R. asiaticus* in late February or March in any good garden soil, in full sun.

R. asiaticus is not reliably hardy. The tubers should be lifted when the foliage has died down, dried and kept in a frost-free place to re-plant in spring. Or they may be grown in a frame and covered with glass in the winter.

Rheum
Rheum alexandrae, height 2½–3 ft (75–90 cm), planting distance 2 ft (60 cm); *R. palmatum* 'Atrosanguineum', 'Rubrum', height 5–8 ft (1·5–2 m), planting distance 3 ft (1 m).

These are plants for the large garden, members of the rhubarb family with enormous leaves that are wonderfully coloured in spring. *R. alexandrae* has never grown well for me, which is particularly sad as the leaves are not too large, fleshy and dark green, and in spring the stems carry papery-look-

Rheum palmatum

ing bracts on spikes 3 ft (90 cm) high, handsome and long-lasting. *R. palmatum* 'Rubrum' and 'Atrosanguineum' produce 6 ft (1·8 m) plumes of flower in pinkish reds and enormous handsome leaves, deep red to purple in April but fading to dull green after flowering.

Arranging. In spring the young leaves are an asset to any foliage arrangement or at the base of a vase of forsythia and white-backed daffodils. The tall flower plumes are useful for large arrangements in May, and bring height and delicacy to a vase of more solid flowers.

Conditioning and preserving. The large new leaves should have their stem ends burnt or dipped in boiling water, and then the whole leaf should be submerged under water overnight. This treatment may need to be repeated after several days, though it depends very much on the maturity of the leaf. The flower stems should also have the ends boiled or burnt, followed by a long drink.

The seed heads dry well if picked after they have formed on the plant and hung upside down until thoroughly dry.

Cultivation. Plant from October to March in any good garden soil, in a sunny site. Water well in dry spells, and give a mulch of suitable material in April. Cut the flower spikes down to ground level in the autumn.

Rodgersia pinnata 'Superba'

Height 3–4 ft (around 1 m), planting distance 2–3 ft (60–90 cm).

Outstandingly handsome foliage plant with red-tinted five-finger leaves, which make a canopy colouring beautifully in autumn, and tall pinkish-red flower spikes appearing in July. It is water-loving and prefers partial shade.

Arranging. If I have only a few of these leaves, then I prefer to save them until the autumn, when they turn such beautiful colours. They bring great distinction to any vase of autumnal colourings especially if arranged in a copper container. The flower panicles are excellent for use in large arrangements.

Conditioning and preserving. The flowers keep better if they are not picked until they are mature. Both flower stems and leaves should have their stem ends dipped in boiling water and then allowed a long drink.

The flower seed heads dry well, but I really prefer to use them fresh in July.

Cultivation. Plant in March or April in any good soil, preferably in a moist situation and in partial shade. Mulch in April, water well in dry spells. Cut down flower spikes to ground level in the autumn.

Rudbeckia fulgida 'Deamii'

Height 2–3 ft (60–90 cm), planting distance 2 ft (60 cm).

This dark-eyed golden daisy flower adds so much to the garden, flowering from July to October when its colour is welcome and always a good flower for picking. In America, where the rudbeckia grows wild in many areas, it may be felt that it is a strange choice for cultivation. However, we are not all so fortunate. I think that *R. fulgida* 'Deamii' is the only variety that I personally wish to grow, but there are many others that add late colour to the border.

Arrangement. The small dark eye is the great attraction for me, and with some black privet or phytolacca berries you have the makings of an interesting arrangement. When in America, I

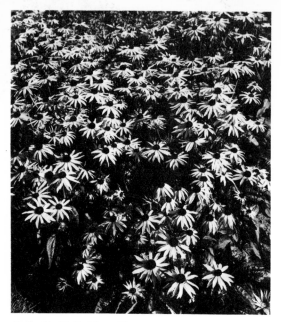

Rudbeckia fulgida 'Deamii'

found that armfuls picked in the wild and arranged to spill out of a trug basket looked superb.

Conditioning and preserving. Bruise the ends of the stems, or dip in a little boiling water, and then allow a long drink.

The single blooms dry well in any of the flower-drying powders and keep a very good colour.

Cultivation. Plant from October to March in full sun or partial shade, in any good garden soil. No staking is normally needed, except in exposed gardens. Cut down to ground level in the autumn.

Salvia

Salvia haematodes, height 3 ft (90 cm), planting distance 2 ft (60 cm); *S. nemorosa* 'Superba', height 2–3 ft (60–90 cm), planting distance 2 ft (60 cm); *S. sclarea* 'Turkestanica', height 2½ ft (75 cm), planting distance 12 in (30 cm); *S. splendens*, height 18 in (45 cm), planting distance 12 in (30 cm).

S. nemorosa 'Superba' gives a lovely patch of colour to the border, and lives a long time, unlike *S. haematodes* which, for me anyway, seems to die out after a few years, though I think it quite the prettiest salvia, with pale lavender flower spikes on stems of about 2–3 ft (60–90 cm). *S. sclarea*

'Turkestanica' also dies out, but seems to seed freely so that once you have it, it will go on reproducing itself. For those of you who live in warm climates, then try a brilliant patch of the scarlet *S. splendens*, often seen in our parks where it is treated as a half-hardy annual and used as a bedding-out plant. It grows on stems slightly shorter than the other varieties of salvia I have mentioned, and has more delicate pendulous flowers.

Arranging. Salvias are useful in mixed summer arrangements. The slim and delicate flower stems make a good background. Stems of the stronger-coloured flowers can be cut short (about 5–6 in (12·5–15 cm) and used as the centre of an arrangement, if this is the colour you particularly want to emphasize. The scarlet *S. splendens* is a wonderful help in clashing red arrangements as it has an outstandingly clear colour and lasts well in water.

Conditioning. All the salvias last better if the stem ends are put into 1 in (2·5 cm) of boiling water, and then given a long deep drink. *S. sclarea* 'Turkestanica' should be handled carefully as it has a very pungent smell that some people find unpleasant—though I find it disappears once the flower has been arranged in the vase.

Cultivation. The biennial species *S. sclarea* is sown very thickly in April in the final position where the plants are to grow. The seedlings are thinned out to leave them 12 in (30 cm) apart, or they may be carefully transplanted. *S. splendens* is a half-hardy annual which must be raised under glass and planted out at the end of May or early in June, when danger of frost is past. The other salvias are hardy perennials and may be planted in any good garden soil from October to March in full sun or in light shade. Cut the stems down to the ground in November.

Scabiosa

Scabiosa caucasica 'Clive Greaves' and 'Miss Willmott', height 2–3 ft (60–90 cm), planting distance 18 in (45 cm).

Open-faced delightful flowers in shades of blue and also white, flowering on stems of 2–3 ft (60–90 cm). I personally find them rather difficult to grow, and so have concentrated on having white ones only, as I am very attached to them and find they are not so easy to buy as the mauve ones, which have become a very popular inexpensive cut flower.

Arranging. During my first-ever television programme, I showed viewers how to make an arrangement of four bunches of scabious in a silver bowl. The intention was to demonstrate that one could make a pretty vase for five shillings (about fifty cents), so there is no need to say how long ago that was! These flowers are ideal for arranging, making an excellent centre, and can be cut with different lengths of stems from 1 ft (30 cm) down to 6 in (15 cm). They can be used to give a recessed effect, which is so important especially if you are making an arrangement of scabious on their own with no unrelated foliage. The white-flowered varieties make a good centre for a mixed white vase or with green foliage.

Conditioning. A long drink in warm water is all they need to make them last very well. If you remember always to cut off the dead blooms on the growing plants, you will find that when arranged the buds will continue to open in water, though paler in colour.

Cultivation. Plant from October to March in any good garden soil, in full sun. The site must be well drained, so on soils that tend to lie wet in winter plant in a raised bed—say 12 in (30 cm) above the soil level. Scabious appreciate a mulch in April. Cut the plants down to ground level in November.

Scrophularia nodosa 'Variegata'
Height 2–3 ft (60–90 cm), planting distance 18 in (45 cm).

The figwort is a wild plant, but this variegated form is highly recommended for the garden, statuesque in form and growing to about 3 ft (90 cm) in height, with leaves blotched and splashed with white.

Arranging. It is advisable to wait until the foliage is mature before picking, and then small pieces can be used in mixed foliage arrangements. Like all variegated plants, it helps to add the necessary light touch for the centre of a foliage group. The small brown flowers are of no value, but after they have developed you can take longer stems of foliage of up to 2 ft (60 cm).

Conditioning. Stem ends should be dipped into

Scabiosa caucasica

Scrophularia nodosa 'Variegata'

boiling water for a few minutes, or singed in a gas flame, and then given a drink in deep water. **Cultivation.** Plant preferably in a moist spot in any ordinary garden soil, from October to March. Water copiously in dry spells on light quick-draining spoil. Nip out the flower spikes as the flowers are insignificant and it is the foliage that is required. Cut down to ground level in November.

Sedum

Sedum aizoon, height and planting distance 12 in (30 cm); *S. alboroseum* 'Variegatum', height 12 in (30 cm), planting distance 2 ft (60 cm); *S.* × 'Autumn Joy', height and planting distance 2 ft (60 cm); *S. maximum* 'Atropur-pureum', height and planting distance 2 ft (60 cm); *S.* 'Ruby Glow', height and planting distance 12 in (30 cm); *S. spectabile* 'Brilliant', height 12–18 in (30–45 cm), planting distance 18 in (45 cm).

One of the best plants for flower arranging and for gardens large and small, growing with little trouble and easily propagated. In fact, when I was first given a piece of *S. maximum* 'Atropur-

Sedum spectabile 'Brilliant'

pureum', I cut the stem just above a pair of leaves, removed the lower pair of leaves from each cutting and planted them in sandy soil. I was soon over-joyed to find I had two well-rooted plants which I still have 15 years later. Of course I have rooted many pieces in this way since, and have a fine collection of sedums; as they also seed freely I have many unusual crosses too. *S. maximum* 'Atropurpureum' is a handsome plant with deep red foliage, growing taller than most other sedums. The fleshy stems have pairs of leaves right up to a flat flower head of tiny stars, and stems, leaves and flowers all have this marvellous red colour. *S. spectabile* 'Brilliant' is a Chinese plant, with glaucous fleshy foliage and attractive soft pink flower heads, making a very good patch of colour in the autumn. One of my favourites is *S.* × 'Autumn Joy' with a flowering period of nearly three months, the flowers starting pink and going a deep red colour, and useful for arranging at all stages. The variegated foliage of *S. albo-roseum* 'Variegatum' is also lovely to use in arrangements and handsome in the border. I grow *S. aizoon* purely for the seed head, though the yellow flowers are quite attractive. Among the smaller rock varieties, *S.* 'Ruby Glow', with dark maroon foliage and good deep pink flowers, looks well grown in pots, with its graceful fall.

Arranging. Sedums are of great value. I start using 'Autumn Joy' in August in the green flower-bud stage, when it mixes with other green leaves; and then later use all sedum flowers as a centre in many arrangements—with the pinks and mauves of asters, for instance, or with apricot-coloured dahlias, gladioli and autumn-coloured foliage, or sprays of rose hips, cotoneaster berried branches and turning beetroot leaves.

Conditioning and preserving. Sedums last well in water with no more treatment than the usual long drink. I always feel they ought to dry well, but in fact they do not, though if used in a vase in late autumn and left there, I find they will actually grow roots in the vase.

Cultivation. Plant from October to April in any good garden soil, in full sun. Preferably give *S. maximum* a moist but not boggy spot. Unless the old flower stems and seed heads are used in arrangements, cut them or snap them off in March or April. The plants appreciate a mulch in April.

Senecio

Senecio cineraria, *S. maritima* (now correctly *S. bicolor*), height 2 ft (60 cm), planting distance 12 in (30 cm); *S. laxifolius*, height and spread 4 ft (1·2 m).

The grey-foliaged cinerarias are worth a corner, for they are useful to cut, and make a grey patch in the border, which creates a restful zone in any scheme of mixed planting. *S. cineraria*, with flannel-textured leaves of deeply cut furry grey, grows into quite a large plant, but then becomes woody and suddenly dies—so I take a few cuttings in July, tucking them into some sand by a stone on the rock garden, and in this way ensure that I always have young plants.

S. laxifolius is most useful for cutting and retains its good grey foliage all winter. It has rounded grey leaves with silver backs, grows to about 3 ft (90 cm) and has a mass of bright yellow daisy flowers in July. Like the cineraria, it tends to die out suddenly, and again it is important always to take a few cuttings.

Arranging. I use the individual leaves of *S. cineraria* at the base of a vase, where they look so well with pale pink roses or garden pinks. Longer stems of *S. laxifolius* are ideal for the background to a winter foliage arrangement.

Conditioning. Dip the cut ends of the stems into boiling water, and then allow a long deep drink. With *S. cineraria*, it is particularly important to see that the hairy part of the leaf does not get into the water, either during conditioning or when arranging. The woody stems of *S. laxifolius* can be hammered before being given a long drink.

Cultivation. *S. cineraria* is almost hardy but is usually treated as a half-hardy annual and planted out each year in spring. Plant *S. laxifolius* from October to March in sun or partial shade in any soil, no matter how poor. It will of course respond to feeding, a mulch in April, and water in dry spells. When the plant becomes rather gaunt or leggy, cut it back really hard, even almost to

ground level if necessary, and it will make copious new growth.

Sisyrinchium striatum   SATIN FLOWER

Height 12–18 in (30–45 cm), planting distance 12 in (30 cm).

The satin flower seeds itself everywhere, but makes splendid groups of grey-green iris-like leaves 12 in (30 cm) high. The flowers, appearing all down the stems of stiff spikes, are straw yellow and last for many weeks. Lovely black seed heads then form, and it is as much for these as for the flowers that I grow this plant.

Arranging. Sadly, the flowers close up at night, both in the garden and when cut, so I pick and use the spikes for only one day. They are useful outline material, and the flowers are a very pleasing soft yellow colour. I use the seed heads all the time, both in their earlier green state and then dried.

Sisyrinchium striatum

Conditioning and preserving. There is no way to keep the little flowers open at night, but for just one day the spikes need no special treatment.

The seed heads dry well if hung upside down. If the stems are put into a glycerine solution, they go a wonderful colour, and like all things treated this way, they are not so brittle to use.

Cultivation. Plant from October to March in full sun, in a well-drained site which has been enriched with peat or leaf-mould. Cut down dead stems and foliage in autumn. Mulch in April.

Smilacina racemosa
Height 2–3 ft (60–90 cm), planting distance 18 in (45 cm).

This plant is related to Solomon's Seal, and has a very similar growth habit, with pairs of leaves on arching stems, but the flower is a sweetly scented fluffy cream spike at the end. In its native North America it grows in the woods, and is a lover of shade and damp, but it also seems to grow well for me in the front of a fairly dry shrub border.

Arranging. These arching sprays add so much to any arrangement: I find them especially useful for giving form in a green group and in their lovely golden yellow autumnal colouring, stems add a downward sweep to a vase of yellows—roses, dahlias and gladioli in a brass pan or bowl.

Conditioning and preserving. Give a long drink in deep water.

The stems take up glycerine quite well: pick before they turn colour, and put the stem ends into a glycerine solution, and you will get a rather limp but well-coloured spray for winter use.

Cultivation. Plant from October to March in good garden soil enriched with compost or well-rotted manure. A moist, partially shaded site is best, and a mulch in April is helpful. Cut down to ground level in November or December.

Stachys lanata   LAMB'S EARS
Height 12 in (30 cm), planting distance 12–18 in (30–45 cm).

A hardy perennial with good grey leaves densely covered in grey wool, and mauve flower spikes, which I personally like to preserve and use in dried arrangements. It provides excellent ground cover, though apt to spread almost too much. There is also a variety named 'Sheila Macqueen' but it has no flowers.

Arranging. The leaves are particularly lovely used individually with pinks for a pink and grey arrangement. Later when the flower spikes form, their dense grey coating makes them ideal for mixing with a vase of old roses. The greys always look well in a silver container.

Conditioning and preserving. It is best to burn the ends of the stems, either in a gas flame or putting the ends into boiling water for a count of twenty, and then give them a long drink, taking care to avoid submerging the hairy leaves, as this causes them to lose their grey colour.

Opposite
1 Delphinium
2 Moluccella
3 Belladonna lily
4 Nerine
5 Rose
6 Dahlia
7 Stock
8 Colchicum
9 *Cineraria maritima*
10 Willow gentian

The graceful stems of willow gentian and grey cineraria outline this autumn arrangement of crocuses, stocks, dahlias and nerines.

When the flower spikes are mature, remove any extra leaves and hang them upside down to dry.

Cultivation. Plant from October to March in any good garden soil, preferably well drained and in full sun. Plants may be grown in partial shade but may be less silvery. Trim the plants over in November or December.

Tellima

Tellima grandiflora, T. grandiflora 'Purpurea', height 18–24 in (45–60 cm), planting distance 18 in (45 cm).

An excellent ground cover. I particularly love the compact clumps of rounded hairy leaves of 'Purpurea', of a lovely rich colour good for picking all the year. The flowers of both forms of this plant have graceful stems of pale green bells. I grow mine in the front of the borders and find they spread well while remaining compact.

Opposite
1 Thalictrum
2 Poppy head
3 *Eryngium giganteum*
4 Thalictrum foliage
5 Hosta
6 *Cineraria maritima*

The simplicity of grey and green seedheads and leaves is ideally suited to this Japanese trough.

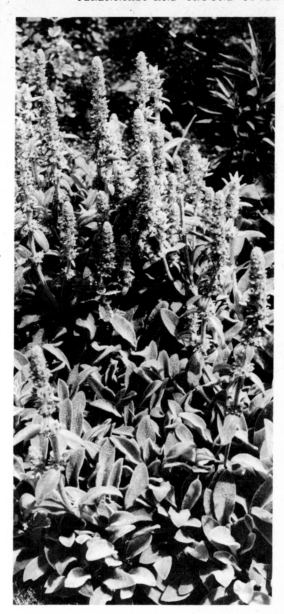

Stachys lanata

Arranging. The leaves act as undershadow at the base of any small arrangement.

Conditioning. As the leaves grow on very short stems, it is best to burn the ends with a lighted match, or in a gas flame, then submerge in cold water for several hours.

Cultivation. Plant from October to March in any reasonably good garden soil, in sun or partial shade. This plant will tolerate dry shade. Cut down faded flower spikes.

Thalictrum

Thalictrum delavayi, height 4–5 ft (1–1·5 m), planting distance 18 in (45 cm); *T. speciosissimum*, height 4–5 ft (1–1·5 m), planting distance 2 ft (60 cm).

T. speciosissimum (*T. glaucum*) is my first choice: with its grey-green columbine-like foliage and fluffy yellow flowers, it is excellent for the back of the border, the leaf colour setting off any plant grown in front of it. *T. delavayi* (usually listed as *T. dipterocarpum*) has delightful nodding heads of mauve flower sprays; it never grows well for me, but is magnificent in the north of Scotland.

Arranging. I like to use the individual leaf sprays, for they are so pretty mixed with roses or delicate pink flowers. I find the flower heads do not last well, but when these are over, the long foliage spikes, of up to 4 ft (1·2 m), are ideal for a large group in July to October. I often use the leaves of *T. delavayi* with columbines, and they look particularly lovely in a glass vase.

Conditioning. The ends of the foliage stems should be dipped into boiling water and then given a long deep drink, but avoid submerging any leaves as this will reduce the grey effect, particularly of *T. speciosissimum*. The flowers need no special treatment, but a long drink is always recommended.

Cultivation. Plant from October to March in full sun or partial shade, in any good garden soil preferably enriched with compost or manure. Mulch in April, and give an occasional feed of soluble fertilizer. Some support of canes will be needed. Cut the plants down to the ground in November or December.

Tiarella cordifolia

Height and planting distance 12 in (30 cm).

I grow this plant mostly as ground cover, though naturally every plant for me has to be useful for arrangements. The small dense clumps of heart-shaped well-marked leaves spread easily, and the leaves turn reddish-bronze in autumn. The masses of white bottle-brush flowers are pretty, but they do not last very well in water.

Arranging. The design and balance of small arrangements are much improved by the addition of these well-marked little leaves at the base.

Conditioning. Submerge the leaves overnight in water.

Cultivation. Plant from October to April in any good garden soil enriched with compost or peat. A moist site is preferable, but if this cannot be provided regular watering should be given in dry spells. Mulch in April. Tidy up the plants in late autumn.

Trollius chinensis   GLOBE FLOWER

Height 2½ ft (75 cm), planting distance 12–18 in (30–45 cm).

The yellows and oranges of globe flowers contrasted with the blue of forget-me-nots and bluebells make a good combination in the garden. The rounded heads are rather like big double buttercups. The only one I would grow is *T. chinensis*, usually listed as *T. ledebouri* as the soft yellow of its flowers is a wonderful blending colour for arrangements.

Arrangement. I love to use these flowers with the first opening buds of *Acer pseudoplatanus* 'Brilliantissimum', some tellima leaves and a few heads of lime-green hellebores or spurge.

Conditioning. Dip the ends of the stems into boiling water before putting them up to their necks in cold water for a long drink.

Cultivation. Plant from October to March in any reasonably good garden soil, in sun or partial shade, in a moist position if possible. In sun, or a dry position, water generously in dry spells, and mulch every April. If the flower stems are cut back after flowering, a second crop may be produced.

Veratrum nigrum

Height 3–4 ft (around 1 m), planting distance 18 in (45 cm).

A rare and extremely handsome plant. The leaves, which unfurl like a fan out of the ground, are pale green with a most unusual pleated effect. The flower spike grows to about 3 ft (90 m), rising out of the centre of the leaf clump, and producing a thick mass of almost black star-like flowers on about the top 9 in (23 cm) of stem. It is worth growing for the leaves alone—at least that is what I tell myself to hide the real disappointment of not getting a flower, as my plant refuses to bloom every year. The veratrum needs sun, but shaded roots, and hates disturbance: in my grandmother's Scottish garden, a number were left to flourish near the raspberry canes, and I have never seen more spectacular plants.

Arranging. These tall handsome precious spikes must be arranged so that they show off their spectacular beauty. Never cut the stems shorter than 2 ft (60 cm), and then, used with stems of black phytolacca seeds, lilies and rounded heads of agapanthus, they are a real joy.

Conditioning and preserving. The ends of the stems must be dipped into boiling water for a few minutes and then allowed a long deep drink. Never pick until the flower is open right up the stem, or you will find that the top of the stem droops, and will never recover. Pick the leaves only after the flower has formed, so that you do not risk taking the growing flower stalk. The foliage is decorative in autumn arranged with gourds and berries, but as the slugs love it, it is often difficult to get a perfect leaf.

The slender flower and seed heads dry well. Once the seed is set, pick the stems and stand them in a little water, and they will then dry off quite quickly.

Cultivation. Plant from October to April, preferably in a moist, semi-shaded site, in any reasonably friable soil. Water in dry spells, and mulch in April. Cut down to the ground in November or December.

Verbascum bombyciferum
Height 4–6 ft (1–2 m), planting distance 2 ft (60 cm).

V. bombyciferum, often listed as *V.* 'Broussa', is a wonderful plant to have for use in arrangements, and in the garden for its spectacularly beautiful grey hairy rosettes of leaves in winter, as good as

any flower. In spring the leaves become more silvery, and covered in woolly down. The flower spike, heavily fleeced with white wool and then studded with small yellow flowers all the way up its branching length, can grow as tall as 12 ft (3·5 m). 'C. L. Adams' is one of the best verbascum cultivars, with deep yellow flowers; but my own favourite is 'Gainsborough', with silvery foliage and the most charming long stems of pale yellow clustered flowers. All verbascums enjoy the sun, and are rewarding because they remain in bloom for about three months.

Arranging. As these are tall erect flowers, they play a background part in any arrangement, and are useful as tall spikes in a summer group. The leaves of the lovely grey *V. bombyciferum* make a base of distinction to a vase at any time of year.

Conditioning and preserving. Stems of the individual leaves should be put into boiling water, and then given a long drink, but avoid submerging the leaf as this will result in destroying the grey effect. The tall young flower stems should be treated in the same way.

The seed heads dry well. When they are set on the plant, pick the stems and hang them upside down to dry. They dry to the most lovely grey colour and are useful as tall stems in a winter flower arrangement.

Cultivation. Plant from October to April in any good well-drained garden soil. Verbascums love full sun, but they make large plants and appreciate plenty of water in dry spells and a mulch in April. Stake the plants in windy gardens, and cut them down to the ground in November or December.

Vinca major
'Variegata', height 12 in (30 cm), planting distance 2 ft (60 cm).

V. major 'Variegata' is the only periwinkle I would grow, as it is the most useful for the flower arranger, with its slightly arching stems of cream and green leaves. All the vincas make excellent ground cover below trees.

Arranging. I find that I use these leaves more in winter than in summer, for they go so well in mixed green arrangements, and there are not so many attractive variegated plants that will hang gracefully for a winter group.

Conditioning. The stem ends must be either burnt or boiled, and then soaked in really deep water overnight.

Cultivation. Plant from October to April, preferably in semi-shade in any good garden soil. Once established they grow luxuriantly, but they appreciate a mulch in April, and plenty of water in dry spells.

Yucca filamentosa   ADAM'S NEEDLE
Height 2–2½ ft (60–75 cm), spread 3–4 ft (around 1 m).

Though many yuccas flower only once in seven years, I would recommend this plant, for you are pretty certain to have at least one bloom every year. I think it looks at its best planted in isolation, when you can really appreciate its statuesque appearance. It grows up to 5 ft (1·5 m) tall, and produces its dramatic tall flower spikes of pendu-

lous ivory bells in July and August. The yucca is a native of California, so not surprisingly it needs lots of sun and a well-drained soil.

Arranging. The tall spikes must be used so that their full height and beauty can be seen. This means a really large group for a really important occasion—I have used them in the Albert Hall where they looked superb. Nevertheless, they could look well in your own home if arranged in a very large shallow container, so that you can see the flower stems in all their glory.

Conditioning. The ends of the stems should be put into boiling water for 2 in (5 cm) up the stem, left in it until the water gets cold, and then given a long deep drink overnight, or even longer if possible since the stems are so woody. Remove any drooping bells as they fade, and in this way you can keep them going a very long time.

Cultivation. Plant from October to March in any garden soil, in full sun. This is an uncomplaining plant that will grow in even poor soils, but it does not like to lie wet in winter.

Yucca filamentosa

Zantedeschia aethiopica

Zantedeschia aethiopica ARUM OR CALLA LILY

Height 2–3 ft (60–90 cm), planting distance 18–24 in (45–60 cm).

I have managed to keep my arum lilies alive and healthy on a south wall now for three winters and look on this as a real triumph. This handsome plant is worth growing just for the magnificent dark-green spade-shaped leaves, though the white arum flower with its yellow central spadix is wonderful in the garden and in the house.

Arranging. Arum lilies are marvellous for a modern arrangement with only line in mind. Using a shallow container, you can make a perfect long-lasting arrangement using a well-shaped background branch, three lilies, each shorter than the last, and two of their own leaves. But I think that the very best use for these lilies is in church decorations, as they show up so well from a great distance in simple altar vases or in a large group. Five lilies will make the centre of any church arrangement. When I was in Kenya once, I was able to use them in armfuls, so I cut them short and made a formal mass arrangement with no stems showing, just lily heads, in a raised black shallow urn. It looked lovely, but I don't suppose I will ever be able to do it again.

Conditioning. The flowers last very well with no special treatment, but the leaves need to be submerged in water overnight. I have found that a weak solution of starch added to the water helps to stiffen them very effectively.

Cultivation. Zantedeschias are hardy in the warmer counties. They seem to thrive best in the deep mud of a pool margin, although they may be grown in a sunny border and covered with straw or bracken in really severe weather. The variety 'Crowborough' seems to be the hardiest. Plant in spring.

Annuals, Bulbs & Corms

Annuals

I have listed only a few annuals that I find particularly useful for flower arranging. Unfortunately most of these are not easily bought as plants, so it is necessary to grow them yourself. However, since I do like to have a few annuals in the border giving colour through July and August, I do buy some young plants, such as antirrhinums, stocks, petunias and verbena, and I find some of the brilliantly coloured geraniums very useful if used as annuals. Plant these in clumps of five plants to make a good splash of colour where some of the early flowers, like perennial poppies, have left a gap. All of these last-named plants may be bought easily from your local nursery or shops.

All of the green plants that I have suggested, as you will see from the photograph on page 132, make an attractive summer arrangement and most of them will dry for use in the winter too. They have been arranged in a shallow glass dish, and all were grown from seed. Nothing could be less expensive and nothing more effective, though of course there is some work involved in growing the plants.

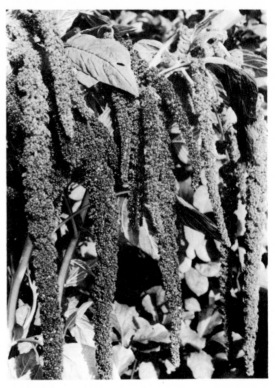

Amaranthus caudatus

Amaranthus

Amaranthus caudatus viridis, height 3–4 ft (around 1 m), planting distance 18 in (45 cm).

This is the green form of Love-lies-Bleeding, which I find so much more attractive than the red. It is worth looking after for if the plant thrives the trusses may be twice as long as normal, and it is a most striking plant to have in the garden. It will seed easily and enjoys a medium or rich soil.

Arranging. The long, trailing tails of green chenille-like trusses make a splendid centre for a summer arrangement, and are equally effective in winter decorations when they have been dried.

Conditioning and preserving. Remove all the leaves immediately after picking, for this plant does not take up enough moisture for both leaves and flowers. Place the stems in really hot water and leave them for several hours before arranging. If you are drying the stems, it is best to place them in shallow water in a warm room and allow to dry. Avoid drying the stems with the elegant, drooping trusses hanging upside down or otherwise they will dry erect!

Cultivation. Sow very thinly in their flowering situation in April in any reasonably fertile soil, and thin the seedlings as they become large enough to handle. Do the thinning in several stages until the plants are at the final distance.

Antirrhinum SNAP DRAGON OR
LION'S MOUTH

'Butterfly', height 2 ft (60 cm), planting distance 12–18 in (30–40 cm); 'Penstemon Flowered', height and planting distance 12 in (30 cm).

As I mentioned earlier antirrhinums are quite easily obtained from nurseries as young plants. The Double varieties and 'Penstemon Flowered' are much more difficult to come by so I recommend you should consider growing them from

Antirrhinum 'Penstemon Flowered'

seed. They have a good colour range with a long flowering period, and 'Penstemon Flowered' has an attractive open tubular flower.

Arranging. Antirrhinums add great charm to a mixed group of summer flowers and look very effective when used by themselves in similar-coloured arrangements. I like to put apricot with flame colours, and white antirrhinums in a white vase can look marvellously dramatic.

Conditioning. They seem to last better if they are placed in warm water. You should carefully remove each floret as it dies and this will keep the flowers looking very fresh.

Cultivation. Try to obtain sturdy, rich green plants, well hardened off, to plant in March or April in any ordinary garden soil, in full sun. Work in compost or manure before planting, and feed several times with a soluble fertilizer during the growing period. When the plants are about 4 in (10 cm) high, pinch out the growing point to make them bushy. Remove dead flowers regularly. Water well in dry spells.

Atriplex

Atriplex hortensis alba, A. hortensis rubra, height 4–4½ ft around 1·3 m), planting distance 2 ft (60 cm).

Atriplex rubra produces tall stems with purple leaves and seeds. It will grow easily from seed and once you have it, it is with you always—as a friend of mine once said, it seeds all the way to the bonfire! *A. alba*, the green form, has green leaves and spinach-like seed heads.

Arranging. The seed heads are extremely useful as part of the background in arrangements. They are equally effective when used with purple tones or with contrasting colours. The green stems mix well in a green group or with blending colours.

Conditioning and preserving. The seed heads dry very well and as soon as the seeds are set it is best to remove every leaf and hang the stems upside down in a warm place to dry.

Cultivation. Sow thinly in any good soil in a sunny spot in March or April. Gradually thin the seedlings until the plants are at their final distance. Water well in dry spells.

Opposite
1 Atriplex
2 Phytolacca
3 Delphinium
4 Colchichum
5 Rose
6 Elder berries
7 Vitis grapes
8 Blackberries
9 Antirrhinum 'Penstemon Flowered'

A near-black and white arrangement of phytolacca and elder berries, sprays of blackberries and white roses.

Cobaea

Cobaea scandens, height 20 ft (6 m), planting distance 2 ft (60 cm).

Better known as Cups and Saucers, Cathedral Bells or Dutchman's Pipe, this plant has lovely trumpets of green turning to pale mauve, and being a climber it is better trained on a fence or wall. If you can train the stems along a wire, you will get a wealth of bloom that may otherwise be difficult to see when the stems grow very high. In its native Mexico cobaea grows freely over fence and wall and it becomes a veritable menace in Australia.

Arranging. These delicate flowers arrange well with mixed greens or as the centre of any vase where their colour is enhancing to the arrange-

Overleaf
1 Moluccella
2 *Cobaea scandens*
3 Sedum
4 Phytolacca
5 Zinnia 'Envy'
6 Nicotiana
7 Atriplex
8 Amaranthus

An arrangement of green annuals. These plants preserve and dry well, which makes them particularly valuable to grow for flower arranging.

ment. The seed heads are striking and look very attractive in a fruit and flower arrangement.

Conditioning and preserving. The trumpet flowers need little conditioning but should be given a drink of warm water in a narrow-necked container when picked. The seed heads do not dry well and I do not recommend your trying to preserve them.

Cultivation. This is a half-hardy perennial but is normally grown as an annual to form a quick screen over trellis, fences, or over a pergola. Sow the seeds in a heated greenhouse in March, prick off the seedlings and plant out when danger of frost is past. Place the seeds edgeways in the soil. This plant will grow in any reasonably fertile soil but appreciates some feeding in summer, and plenty of water in dry spells.

Page 133
1 Acanthus
2 Hollyhock
3 Agapanthus
4 Delphinium
5 Hydrangea

The blue of this English delftware vase is reflected in the blues of hydrangeas and agapanthus in this informal arrangement. The rounded heads of these flowers are set off by the tall acanthus spikes.

Opposite
1 Nicotiana
2 Gladiolus
3 Dahlia
4 Rose
5 Antirrhinum

Copper containers with their polished surfaces are particularly useful for arrangements of orange flowers with reds and yellows. The green of the foliage and the nicotiana helps blend the brighter colours of roses and dahlias.

Moluccella   BELLS OF IRELAND

Moluccella laevis, height 2 ft (60 cm), planting distance 9 in (23 cm).

Known as the Shell Flower and in Australia as Molucca Balm. Moluccella carries a spike of pale green bell-shaped bracts, and the flower is the small eye in the centre of the bell. The seeds are a little difficult to germinate without the help of a really hot summer, and artificial heat may be needed to start them off.

Arranging. This plant is ideal for flower arranging in all stages of growth. The stems take on lovely natural curves and when the small leaves are removed they last so well that they will actually dry to a delightful cream colour while in an arrangement. They look good alone or with almost any colour combinations.

Conditioning and preserving. Remove the leaves, and the stems will last extremely well in water. They dry beautifully, either out of doors on the plant if the weather is really hot, or in an arrangement in water. They preserve best of all in a solution of glycerine and water. Leave the stems for four or five days and then remove them from the glycerine and hang upside down for a few days. In this way the stems stay quite firm and they turn a delightful parchment colour, with an oily feel. The glycerine treatment helps to ensure that the bells do not drop and makes the stems less brittle so that they are easier to arrange. In America, in order to retain the colour, a little green dye is added to the glycerine which results in an attractive, natural-looking green stem.

Cultivation. Moluccella will grow in any reasonably fertile garden soil, and preferably in full sun. Sow the seed under glass in March, prick off the seedlings, and after hardening them off in a cold frame plant them out towards the end of May.

Or sow the seed in late April in the open ground, and thin the seedlings gradually to leave them at their final distance.

Nicotiana TOBACCO PLANT

Nicotiana affinis (*N. alata*) 'Lime Green', height 2–3 ft (60–90 cm), planting distance 12 in (30 cm).

The green tobacco, growing to 2 ft (60 cm) high or more and wonderful lime-green in colour, is something I cannot wait for once the moluccella is over. The white form, which has a lovely perfume at night, is superb when planted near the house for filling the evening with its delicious scent. Green tobacco is easily grown but it is difficult to buy in plant form, although the coloured varieties are easily obtainable.

Arranging. The lime colour harmonizes with any colour scheme from pinks and reds to white and cream and I find it invaluable for all sorts of arrangements.

Conditioning and preserving. Nicotiana lasts well in water with little more than a long drink of warm water for an hour or so after picking. Unfortunately there is no means of preserving other than by drying the individual flowers in silica gel.

Cultivation. Sow the seed in March in a heated greenhouse, harden off the seedlings, and plant out when danger of frost is past—at the end of May or early in June. Plant in full sun or light shade in any reasonably fertile soil. Water well in dry spells.

Zinnia

Zinnia elegans 'Envy', height 2–2½ ft (60–75 cm), planting distance 12 in (30 cm).

If you find zinnias do well in your garden, the colours will be superb and you must, of course, grow them. I find them difficult but 'Envy' flourishes and adds colour to the border. As sun lovers zinnias need full sun and like a well-drained soil.

Arranging. 'Envy' makes a wonderful centre to

any green arrangement, and if you grow other varieties as well they are excellent in mixed arrangements for late summer and the autumn.

Conditioning and preserving. The ends of the stems should be placed in boiling water and then allowed a long drink. If the stems are brittle, it is advisable to put a firm florists' wire right up the stem. (Very often when zinnias arrive in the market this has already been done.)

You can preserve zinnias beautifully by removing the stems completely and replacing them with florists' wire; the flowers should be laid in a box of preserving powder. They keep their colour very well and are ideal in winter arrangements.

Cultivation. Sow the seeds under glass in March, prick out and harden off the seedlings, and plant them out at the end of May or early June when danger of frost is past. Or seed may be sown direct in a well-prepared seed bed in mid to late May, and the seedlings thinned out gradually to their final distance. Zinnias enjoy good fertile soil and plenty of water in dry weather.

Zinnia elegans 'Envy'

136

Bulbs and corms

It is possible to create a fantastic spring show in your garden using almost all bulbs, and indeed many gardens are at their best then; but this is, of course, a very extravagant way of gardening. I could never afford to buy many bulbs at any one time, so I have had to collect gradually, and have bought a few more each year. I think the bulbs you should buy first are the ones that will give you a quick show: any of the daffodil and narcissi group are very rewarding as they increase each year, so if you start off with only twelve bulbs, very soon they will have doubled. Tulips are another good buy and the Cottage and hybrid Darwin types will flower for many years; I would recommend that you avoid the rather special doubles and exotics at first.

For the rock or paved garden, and for sink areas, the small *Iris reticulata* increase well, and so do grape hyacinths, scillas and snowdrops. Crocus seem to have more enemies—mice are very partial to them—and so you may have to replace these more frequently. If you have a chalky soil, then it is well worth while buying some bedding hyacinths, as they seem to enjoy chalk and increase very well. I always plant out any of the bulbs I have in the house, and now have quite a good collection from these alone. I would certainly buy a few colchicum, or autumn crocus, as these flower at a time when there is little colour. Nerines are another good autumn-flowering bulb. It really all boils down to what your budget is, and how much you feel you can lay out in the early years.

As bulbs last pretty well with no special treatment, I am omitting the conditioning and preserving sections from the following plant details, but here are some general principles. Most flowers grown from bulbs prefer shallow water, and I have found that daffodils definitely last better in a shallow container. Like all flowers, though, as soon as possible after picking, the stems should be put in deep water for an hour or so. A little sugar in the water used for an arrangement seems to help some bulbous subjects. Avoid singeing or boiling as the stems are very delicate and soon burn; this damage creeps up the stems quickly, making them soft and unmanageable.

The flower heads of daffodils, snowdrops, aconites and grape hyacinths can be preserved in flower-drying powder, but there is no way of preserving the flowers from most bulbs.

If you have to go any distance with a bunch of daffodils or hyacinths or snowdrops—in fact any flowering bulb—it is best to put them into an airtight polythene bag, where they will last very well.

Allium

Allium caeruleum (*A. azureum*), height 2 ft (60 cm), planting distance 6 in (15 cm); *A. giganteum*, height 4 ft (1·2 m), planting distance 12 in (30 cm); *A. ostrowskianum*, height 12 in (30 cm), planting distance 3–4 in (7·5–10 cm); *A. rosenbachianum*, height 2 ft (60 cm), planting distance 6–12 in (15–30 cm); *A. roseum* 'Grandiflorum', height 12 in (30 cm), planting distance 4–6 in (10–15 cm); *A. siculum*, height 2–4 ft (60 cm–1·2 m), planting distance 12 in (30 cm).

Onion, leek and garlic all belong to this family, and the species grown for their flowers are also faintly onion-scented, which may be offputting for some people, but they are good as cut flowers despite this.

My favourite is *A. siculum* from Sicily, its large dark-red bell-like flowers with the outer petals striped in blue-green, borne on curving 3 ft (90 cm) stems. The loose umbels of up to thirty flowers, appearing in May and June, are very unusual and striking. The shorter *A. caeruleum* has rounded heads of deep-blue flowers in June and July. Others I would recommend are *A. giganteum*, a real giant with huge heads of purple flowers on 4 ft (1·2 m) stems; *A. rosenbachianum*, one of the best for arranging with large heads of purple-lilac flowers; *A. ostrowskianum*, with short stems of bright pink flowers, excellent for the rock garden; and *A. roseum* 'Grandiflorum', a little taller with small rounded purple flowers, which dry so well and retain their colour all winter.

Arranging. These rounded heads are useful for putting into summer mixed groups, and are marvellous to use when dried. They dry best if left in very shallow water in a warm place, or if hung upside down. One of the most striking arrangements I ever saw was a mobile made from three heads of the giant allium, and we awarded it first prize at the great Toronto show.

Cultivation. Plant from September to November —the earlier the better—in any good well-drained soil, in sun in an open bed, or among shrubs or herbaceous plants. Mulch and give some soluble feed for the first year or two until the bulbs are well established. Remove flower heads as they fade.

Chionodoxa gigantea GLORY OF THE SNOW

Height 8 in (20 cm), planting distance 4 in (10 cm).

Little star-shaped flowers which I find invaluable for that touch of blue that is so important for a mixed arrangement in early spring, or for a moss garden. My grandmother had what she called her 'blue bed'—a flower bed of about 10 ft by 4 ft (3 m by 1.2 m) against the end of the house, entirely filled with a mixture of chionodoxa and scilla, and a solid mass of blue when in flower. I have no idea how long it took to reach this size, but it was quite superb, and people came from miles around just to see it as soon as the snow had gone.

Arranging. Chionodoxa looks splendid in groups in a moss garden.

Cultivation. Plant in September to November— the earlier the better—in full sun in ordinary but well-drained garden soil. No further attention is needed, but if, after some years, the clumps of bulbs become congested, they should be lifted, divided, and replanted.

Colchicum AUTUMN CROCUS

Colchicum autumnale, height 6 in (15 cm), planting distance 9 in (23 cm).

Delightful autumn-flowering bulb that produces single and double crocus-like flowers in white and

Colchicum

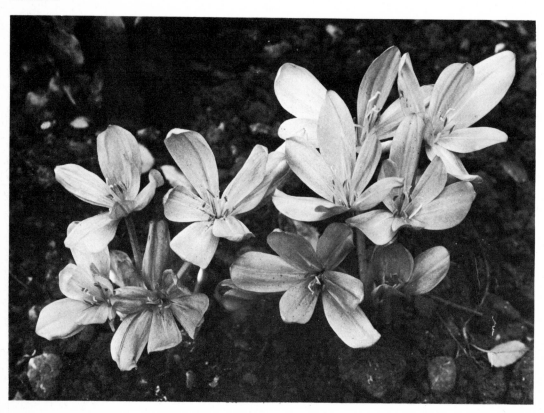

varying shades of purple. The flowers appear straight out of the ground before the leaves, making a lovely display. The leaves are rather unsightly, so it is best to plant colchicum under azaleas or round specimen trees.

Arranging. The large white colchicum is one of the flowers that is superb to arrange, looking best in a shallow silver bowl or entrée dish, arranged on a pinholder which can be hidden by a piece of coral or moss; in this way they need no unrelated foliage. The purple ones need the help of some other flowers, and are prettiest mixed with gentian, nerines, the last pink roses and some *Erica* 'H. E. Beale'.

Cultivation. Plant in August or September in any reasonable soil, in full sun. Remove the dead leaves in June or July, and if desired, lift and transplant the bulbs.

Crocus

Crocus biflorus, C. chrysanthus, C. sieberi, C. tomasinianus, height 4 in (10 cm), planting distance 3–4 in (7·5–10 cm).

Nothing makes a warmer or more attractive show in the garden than these early flowering spring bulbs. The ordinary golden-yellow is one of my favourite colours, for it gives such a glow on a chilly but bright spring day. The crocus naturalizes well in grass and makes a good underplanting subject for the shrub border.

The species crocus are the best of all: if left undisturbed they increase well and are ideal for rock garden and sinks. Among the most attractive are *C. biflorus,* the flowers white, feathered blue; *C. sieberi,* delicate blue with a golden throat; *C. tomasinianus,* a variety that increases and hybridizes well, producing a wide range of mauves, of which 'Whitwell Purple' is a good example; and many cultivars of *C. chrysanthus,* such as 'E. A. Bowles', canary yellow with bronze veining; 'Zwanenburg Bronze', an unusual bronze yellow; 'Golden Bunch', the earliest of all to flower; and 'Snow Bunting', white with a yellow throat.

Arranging. Perhaps the crocus is not one of the best flowers for the flower arranger, but I love to use them in a moss garden; and a bowl of white crocus grown in stones looks lovely in the house in January.

Cultivation. Plant in September, October or November, the earlier the better, in any good garden soil, even in grass. Plant the corms about 3 in (7·5 cm) deep. Remove the old foliage at the end of June. When the clumps become congested after a few years, lift them after the foliage has died down, separate the corms, and replant.

Cyclamen

Cyclamen coum, C. neapolitanum, C. repandum, height 4 in (10 cm), planting distance 4–6 in (10–15 cm).

Cyclamen are ideal for planting under silver birch, or in short grass, or in a rockery. *C. coum* produces flowers all winter, but is at its loveliest in spring, with deep red flowers. *C. repandum* has fragrant flowers in an attractive rose colour and well-marbled leaves. *C. neapolitanum* is perhaps the best known autumn-flowering cyclamen, and the white form is my favourite, producing small flowers on stems of not more than 3 or 4 in (7·5–10 cm).

Arranging. These tiny flowers need care in arranging as they can very easily be overshadowed. I use the flowers and leaves in really miniature arrangements, but I think it is almost best to arrange them on their own in a very small vase.

Cultivation. These hardy cyclamen thrive best in semi-shade, in any good soil that has been enriched with peat or leaf-mould. Dry corms are best planted in September or October, but better results are usually obtained if green pot-grown plants can be purchased and planted in March or April. The ideal spot for these cyclamen is in a lightly shaded woodland site with deep rich soil.

Dahlia

Pompons, Decorative and Cactus classes, height 1–4½ ft (30 cm–1·5 m), planting distance 18–24 in (45–60 cm).

The Pompon or Decorative types of dahlia are the best for flower arranging; the large-headed flowers are so difficult to arrange. There is an enormous range of colours available, so choose those shades which will blend best in your house. I particularly like the apricot shades for their warmth. 'Baseball' is a compact small white, 'Ponos' a clear pink, and for vivid red my choice would be 'Hawaii'. In the Decorative and Cactus classes 'Polar Beauty' is a good white, while 'Apricot Waverley Pearl' is one I find invaluable. 'Newby' and 'New Church' are both peach-coloured; 'Jescot Jim' is a good clear yellow, and 'Jescot Buttercup' a paler and more delicate colour; 'Delicious' and 'Jerry Hoek' are reliable pinks; 'Cherry Ripe', 'Hockley Maroon' and 'Doris Day' are good reds. 'Chorus Girl' is a lilac pink, which can be a useful blending colour. However small your garden may be you ought to grow some dahlias. For the last two years instead of lifting the tubers in the late autumn I have covered them with polythene and straw and have left them undisturbed in the ground. You may well lose some in a hard winter, but as I always used to lose some when I took them up I feel the risk is justified!

Arranging. Dahlias invariably flower well and one can pick them almost every day, so I like to have them in abundance in the house—large bowls of apricot and red and yellow and white, depending on the setting. I find the pink dahlias blend particularly well with nerines and mauve asters and add a splendid colour and glow to a red arrangement.

Conditioning and preserving. Dahlias like a little sugar in the water, but it is best to add an aspirin too as this helps to discourage algae from forming. Put the ends of the stems into a little boiling water and then give them a long drink. I noticed as early as 1959 that they had boiled all the stems of the dahlias which I bought in Sydney, Australia, where dahlias are widely grown and used for flower arrangements. The small Pompons preserve well in any flower-drying powder but, as usual, they must be kept in a dry atmosphere or they will quickly lose their colour.

Cultivation. Plant late May or early June. The taller varieties will need staking. When the plants are about 12 in (30 cm) high nip out the growing point to encourage the production of side shoots.

Mulch and water generously in dry spells and give foliar feeds two or three times after planting at fortnightly intervals. Lift the tubers in the autumn and store in a frost-free place.

Eranthis hyemalis   WINTER ACONITE
Height 4 in (10 cm), planting distance 3 in (7.5 cm).

A hardy tuberous-rooted perennial, this small, buttercup-like flower surrounded by a ruff of green heralds the spring, and I must include it here for that reason. It is best propagated by division during the summer when a leaf is showing, for the dry bulbs are difficult to establish.

Arranging. Winter aconites have very short stems, but they are ideal for a small moss garden, as they give it that invaluable touch of yellow.

Cultivation. Plant in September to November in full sun or in partial shade. No further attention is needed.

Erythronium dens-canis
'Kondo', 'Lilac Wonder' and 'Pagoda', height and planting distance 6 in (15 cm).

Erythronium, or dog's tooth violet, is a corm worthy of a place in any garden, producing fragile little flowers in March and April. 'Kondo' may be one of the most popular varieties, but for me 'Pagoda' is best of all, the long stems carrying four or five large canary-gold flowers, the flat petals turned up at the tips, revealing conspicuous cinnamon antlers—a charming and graceful plant. 'Lilac Wonder' is probably the most widely grown, and I have seen a bank in North Wales covered with these flowers—a wonderful sight.

Arranging. 'Pagoda' is enchanting by itself arranged in a slim wine glass—a lovely way to see and enjoy this flower. Both pink and white-flowered forms enhance any vase of little spring flowers.

Cultivation. Plant from September to November, preferably in a semi-shaded and fairly moist situation. Erythroniums prefer a rich, moisture-retentive soil.

Fritillaria

Fritillaria caucasica, height and planting distance 12 in (30 cm); *F. imperialis*, height 2–3 ft (60–90 cm), planting distance 12 in (30 cm); *F. meleagris*, height 12–18 in (30–45 cm), planting distance 6 in (15 cm).

The large bulb of the Crown Imperial, *F. imperialis*, produces a circle of elegant bell-shaped flowers in orange or yellow surmounted by the 'crown', a tuft of leaves resembling a pineapple. It makes a tall and handsome plant for the back of the border particularly valuable because it flowers so early, and is well worth growing for use in large groups.

In contrast, *F. meleagris* stands not more than 18 in (45 cm) high with nodding heads chequered in pale and deep purple. Another small fritillary is one of the best for flower arranging: *F. caucasica* comes from Turkey and produces quite enchanting deep maroon-coloured bells, yellowish inside and with a silvery bloom on the outside petals.

Arranging. The large stems of Crown Imperial look well arranged alone in a copper or wood container. They take on graceful curves in water, and are ideal for a large church group, or in an arrangement inspired by a Flemish flower painting, in which they frequently appear. The tiny fritillaries add a distinctive charm to a small vase of early species tulips, grape hyacinths, small widow iris (*Hermodactylus tuberosa*) and tellima leaves.

Cultivation. Plant from September to November in any well-drained fertile soil, in full sun, although *F. imperialis* will grow in partial shade. Cut stems down to the ground as they die.

Galanthus   SNOWDROP

Height 6–8 in (15–20 cm), planting distance 3–4 in (7.5–10 cm).

I think everyone must know the snowdrop: no garden would be complete without them. They are the first brave flowers to weather the snow, so good for planting in woodland or beneath shrubs or along the base of a hedge where they remain undisturbed, and they increase all the time. I remember Beverley Nichols saying that he always dug up some to have in a bowl in the house in the early spring, and that it was the best treatment they could have had, for before re-planting he split the bulbs up and put some into another part of the garden.

Arranging. A whole mass of snowdrops dug out of the garden and planted in a big bowl not only looks marvellous but lasts exceedingly well. However, I also like to use them in a moss garden in clumps, with crocus, scilla and small pieces of pussy willow or blossom.

Cultivation. Plant bulbs in October or as soon after as possible. They succeed in grass in the open, under trees or in light woodland, as well as in the rock garden or in the front of a border. If snowdrops have to be moved, or the clumps divided, do this immediately after flowering.

Gladiolus

Height 2–4 ft (60 cm–1.2 m), planting distance 4–6 in (10–15 cm).

Half-hardy corms, producing vigorous spikes of flowers in a wide variety of colours. This is one of the most useful flowers for arranging, and personally I grow them in a cutting area so that I can take as many as I need at any time. If you are limited for space, these are among the few flowers I think it is worth buying to arrange, especially as they are available at florists almost all the year round.

Arranging. Gladioli are useful at all times for their stiff upright stems, which provide the outline that is so important, especially for large arrangements—in white for weddings; pink in vases of mixed pinks and blues perhaps; all shades of red in mixed and 'clashing' reds; 'Woodpecker' for green arrangements. They should never be cut short, but always used with at least 6 in (15 cm) of stem. Picked when in bud with just a touch of colour showing, and left in a cool place, they will remain at that stage for a long time, and will then come out in warm water overnight. I never take off the top buds, as I like the natural curving ends, though many people believe that it is only by removing the buds at the tip that you can ensure every floret will open fully. I am sure that they do this in any case; but it is very important to remove faded florets from the main stem, as these do make the flower look dead.

Cultivation. Plant in full sun in any good garden soil enriched with manure or compost, from mid-March to late April. There are varieties that flower early, in mid-season, or late. By planting several batches of your favourite varieties at fortnightly intervals you can spread the supply of flowers over a long period. Plant the corms 4–6 in (10–15 cm) deep, and give support of canes in exposed gardens. Feed and water in summer. Gladioli need copious supplies of water. Lift the plants when the flowers are over in October, dry the corms, and store in a frost-free room or building.

Hyacinthus   HYACINTH
Height and planting distance 9 in (23 cm).

Muscari   GRAPE HYACINTH
Height 8–10 in (20–25 cm), planting distance 4 in (10 cm).

With their fragrant spikes of pink, white or blue flowers, hyacinths are among the most rewarding flowers to grow, naturalizing well, particularly in light chalky soils.

Grape hyacinths make excellent underplanting for magnolias and late-flowering shrubs.

Arranging. Hyacinths are among the best bulbs for planting into bowls in the autumn so that you can have their sweetly scented flowers in the house in midwinter. I prefer not to mix the colours, but to use containers as large as I can afford, each filled with hyacinths of one colour. I love using them as cut flowers, and though it is possible to buy them in bunches these days, I find I can nearly always pick from my bowls, for once the main flowering is over, there are often a few stragglers left that can best be used in a vase of cut flowers. If you can get a really large number of stems, there is one arrangement that is quite superb, and that is an enormous vase just of hyacinths, either all in one colour, or in mixed colours, in which case it is important to group the flowers—say five each of pink, white, blue and mauve.

The little grape hyacinths are at their most effective in tiny spring arrangements or in a moss garden.

Cultivation. Hyacinths, forms of *H. orientalis*, are very expensive nowadays and many people only use them to grow in bowls and then plant them in the garden after flowering. They grow in full sun or light shade, in any reasonably good soil, and make a good edging to a rose bed or shrub border.

Grape hyacinths, muscari, grow in sun or partial shade in any good garden soil.

Plant hyacinths and muscari bulbs in October or as soon after as possible. Muscari naturalize so well by self-sown seed that they may become a nuisance in a rock garden, for example.

Leucojum   SUMMER SNOWFLAKE
Leucojum aestivum, height 2 ft (60 cm), planting distance 8 in (20 cm).

After the snowdrops come the snowflakes, with hanging heads like a larger and more sturdy snowdrop, the attractive little bells tipped with green.

Arranging. They look charming in groups in a moss garden and are very useful for adding to a green and white early spring arrangement.

Cultivation. Plant in September or October if possible, in any good soil. Lift the clumps and divide them after flowering if they become overcrowded and produce leaves but few flowers.

Lilium   LILY
Lilium candidum, height 4 ft (1·2 m), planting distance 12 in (30 cm); *L. regale*, height 4–6 ft (1–2 m), planting distance 12 in (30 cm); *L. martagon*, height 4–5 ft (1–1·5 m), planting distance 8–10 in (20–25 cm); *L. testaceum*, height 5–6 ft (1·5–2 m), planting distance 6–8 in (15–20 cm); De Graaf Hybrids, height 3–6 ft (1–2 m), planting distance 6–12 in (15–30 cm).

L. candidum, the Madonna lily, is one of my favourites. A group makes a good show in the

Opposite
A modern Japanese container framing three white peony blooms.

garden and the flowers enjoy the warmth of a south wall, though they seem to flourish in many cottage gardens. *L. regale* is one of the most popular of all, lasting well and continuing to bloom year after year; the creamy flowers, backed with pink, are ideal in so many flower arrangements. *L. martagon*, white and purple, has a strange scent which makes it less popular, though I love it. All these are the standard lilies, but the American De Graaf hybrids have introduced a whole new colour range. From the yellow 'Limelight' to the pink of 'Pink Perfection' and the green and black of 'Black Magic' there is a wide choice. For reliability you cannot improve upon 'Enchantment' which I have grown with little or no trouble for many years.

Arranging. All lilies have a quality, from the texture of that lovely trumpet to the way they hold their heads, that makes them superb for flower arranging. They seem to show up from a long distance better than any other flower, which makes them particularly valuable for church flower arrangements. Two lily heads make a focal point in the centre of the vase which is difficult to achieve in any other way. My favourite combination is to have lilies of any shade arranged with a background of stripped lime (branches of lime tree flowers with the leaves removed).

Conditioning and preserving. Care in handling is very important as the petals bruise easily; cut the stems on a slant and place in warm water for several hours. The seed heads of *L. regale* dry well, though it is not very good for the bulbs to keep the seed heads on the stems. However, it is well worth while trying one, as the stems have a candelabra-like seed head which will last all winter.

Cultivation. Plant from October to March in well-drained good garden soil enriched with peat,

Lilium candidum

Opposite
1 Cynara
2 Moluccella
3 Eryngium
4 Old man's beard

Dried seedheads and preserved foliage in a brown alabaster vase make a good standby when flowers are scarce. Nothing could be more useful, as the arrangement stands for several months and still looks attractive. A few fresh flowers could be added after Christmas, however, to give a little extra colour. The artichoke head makes an unusual focal point in the centre of the arrangement.

well-rotted manure or garden compost. Lilies generally succeed in sun or partial shade, and will flower rather later in the shaded sites. *L. candidum* and *L. martagon* will put up with some lime in the soil. A free-draining soil is essential, and if the ground lies wet in winter plant your lilies in raised beds. A slightly sloping site is best. Plant the bulbs about 6 in (15 cm) deep. Give a mulch of manure, peat or compost in spring. Cut down the stems to the ground in late autumn.

Narcissus DAFFODIL, NARCISSUS, JONQUIL
Height up to 18–20 in (45–50 cm), planting distance 4–6 in (10–15 cm).

Heralds of spring and among our best-loved bulbs: what would any garden be without them? The yellow trumpet flowers of daffodils look their best when naturalized in grass or as underplanting for trees and shrubs; others, like the miniature species, are ideal for the rock garden. There are so many species and varieties that it is possible to have some in bloom over a period of almost three months.

Among the modern daffodils, I think the short trumpet varieties are the best for arranging, such as 'Polindra', 'Binkie', 'Green Island' and 'Fermoy'. 'Geranium' and 'Paper White' are both excellent for forcing early. White trumpet and unusual cultivars include: 'Mount Hood', 'Beersheba', 'Devon Loch'. Faintly pink ones are 'Mrs R. O. Backhouse' and 'Salmon Trout'. A good double white is 'Snowball' ('Shirley Temple'); 'Spellbinder' is a superb greenish colour; 'Cherie' carries three heads to a stem, and is cream-buff. For early flowering I would never be without 'February Gold' or 'March Sunshine'.

For the rock garden the miniature species I would recommend are *N. bulbocodium* and *N. bulbocodium* 'Conspicuus' (hoop petticoat), *N. cyclamineus*, *N.* × *hawera*, *N. triandrus* 'Albus' (Angel's Tears). These look effective in the garden and arrange well, too.

Arranging. Daffodils and narcissi last better if arranged in shallow water, and I enjoy them best when they look as if they are growing naturally. So I often use a shallow container, cover the netting and mechanics with a layer of moss, and make the arrangement with one attractive branch of catkin or blossom and a group of daffodils. When they are plentiful and inexpensive, they also look delightful massed into a basket.

Cultivation. Plant in September or October for preference, or as soon after as possible. Narcissi succeed in any good garden soil, especially if it is fairly moisture retentive, although the bulbs do not like being waterlogged. They may be grown in full sun or light shade. See that they get plenty of water if the weather is dry between the time the flowers fade and the leaves begin to die down. Spraying the leaves with a foliar feed several times at 10 day intervals, from mid-April onwards, helps to encourage offset bulbs to grow to flowering size more quickly. Remove the dead heads as the flowers fade to prevent seed formation.

Nerine bowdenii
Height 2 ft (60 cm), planting distance 6 in (15 cm).

The hardiest of these decorative South African bulbs is *N. bowdenii*, with pale pink flowers borne in umbels on slender stems, its greatest asset being that it flowers in September and October. This nerine does well on a south wall, liking the shelter and warmth and increasing well after it has been established for a few years. I also have a white-flowered variety which I hope I can keep as it is not quite so hardy.

Arranging. Nerines mix well with the last pieces of pink and blue out of the border, but also look good alone with a dramatic stem of lichen-covered branch. The flowers should be used with stems never shorter than 5 in (13 cm) to be sure of showing off their elegant form.

Cultivation. Plant in spring or August, preferably in a border at the foot of a south-facing wall, in any good but well-drained soil. The bulbs tend to draw themselves on to the surface of the ground, and while they will withstand a normal winter, they may be killed in a very severe one. So it is worth while covering them with a foot of peat in November, removing it in spring so that the sun may reach the bulbs.

Nerine bowdenii

Tulipa   TULIP

Late or Cottage, Darwin, Parrot, Doubles, *Tulipa viridiflora*, height 2–2½ ft (60–75 cm), planting distance 6 in (15 cm).

Cottage tulips flower in late spring and are good for both bedding out and cutting. There are numerous varieties of the popular Darwin tulips, which are also excellent for bedding out and cutting. One tulip I would never be without is the early flowering 'Apricot Beauty'. The delicate lily flowered tulips are lovely to arrange, for they have the most graceful lines. Among the early Doubles 'Tea Rose' is a delightful cream blushed pink; from the late Doubles I would single out the May-flowering 'Mount Tacoma' (white),

'Eros' (pink), and 'Lilac Time' (mauve). These give a marvellous focal point to any large group. The green tulips, *T. viridiflora*, are splendid for arranging and 'Artist', which has apricot stripes, adds an unusual touch of interest to any vase. Parrot tulips with their strange markings look strikingly original in arrangements. The early tulips for the rock garden add a bright splash of colour in the winter days both in the garden and in the house; *T. hageri* is orange striped with green and *T. linifolia* is coloured a remarkable red and grey.

Arranging. Tulips arrange well on their own or when mixed with unrelated foliage, such as hornbeam catkins or willow, as background. They blend with any colour scheme through having such a wide range of colours. A few double whites will make an outstanding centre in a large group for a white wedding in May.

Conditioning. Cut off the white ends of the stems, wrap the bunch in newspaper with all the heads tightly together and put in deep warm water for several hours. I have found that pricking with a pin right under the head and through the stem releases the air bubble which allows the tulip to drink more easily and has the effect of making it last much longer.

Cultivation. Plant tulips from September to December in any good well-drained garden soil, in full sun. Some varieties will remain in the ground and flower for years, others dwindle away. If they are to be grown mainly for cutting, they may be planted in a patch in the vegetable plot or 'cutting garden', and left to grow for several years. Or they may be lifted after flowering, laid in the ground in a shallow trench, and the bulbs lifted when the leaves and stems have died down. Dry the bulbs off and store in a cool shed until planting time.

Arranging

In this book I have concentrated on plants from your garden that can be used for flower arranging all the year round, and this results in a rather special approach to the actual design of the arrangements. With each changing season the arrangements will change too, in shape, texture and type: you will make flowing massed or mixed arrangements in midsummer when there is plenty of material available, and more simple, economical groups in the winter and early spring.

Naturally, in January you will have to search your garden for bits and pieces, but if it has been a mild winter, it is amazing what you can find to pick, and it is generally possible to make a good all-green arrangement based on one unusual piece, such as a branch of *Garrya elliptica* with catkins, or of contorted willow or hazel, with some leaves of bergenia and the variegated euonymus—a real standby. Camellia foliage is a very special asset in midwinter, and this is also when aucuba comes into its own.

Very early in the year forsythia stems can be brought into the house for forcing, and so can branches of flowering currant. Catkined branches of hazel also force well, and provide excellent outline shape for any arrangement. The earliest flowering trees and shrubs—*Viburnum fragrans*, *Hamamelis mollis* and Winter Sweet, and that wonderful tree that blooms so well off and on all winter, *Prunus subhirtella* 'Autumnalis'—make good outline material and often bring scent into the house too. They can also be used to provide the tall stems for a moss garden, which is an arrangement in a shallow dish where layers of wire netting are covered with fresh moss (it is always a good idea to collect the moss well before Christmas, when it is plentiful, and keep it in a polythene bag). After positioning the flowering branch, you can place into the moss small bunches of snowdrops, aconites, crocus and so on. I often make the first moss garden of the year in a saucer, and use a larger container as the flowers and other material become more abundant.

There are very few tall flowers in the garden at this time of year, so if you want an arrangement for some special occasion, then it means buying a few flowers, at any rate until the early daffodils appear.

By the time early summer arrives you should have plenty to pick for your arrangements. Sometimes the fewer the flowers available, the better the arrangements turn out to be. It can be very confusing to have such a wealth of material that you don't know where to start, and generally speaking mass arrangements are more difficult to do well. It is only possible to do a vase of all one type of flower when there is a profusion, as with daffodils, roses, sweet peas or dahlias. Except in those cases, you will nearly always have to tackle a vase using many different and unrelated flowers and foliage. One word of advice: try to make every flower show as an individual subject. If you always remember this simple principle, you will never be guilty of overcrowding.

A 'mixed green' group is without doubt one of the most effective and attractive types of arrangement at any time of year. It can be created from a very few leaves or using a great mass of foliage in different colours—yellows and greys as well as all the greens—and perhaps with green flowers or seed heads added. These arrangements vary in shape and texture more than any other kind of group.

Through the winter I find that I use more and more dried arrangements, but I think it is best of all if you can use part dried and part fresh material. A few fresh chrysanthemums help a dried group, and later some stems of green hellebore are a wonderful addition. The fresh flower stems can be put into a small separate container within the larger vase of drieds, but often I simply put water in with the dried flowers. It does no harm, and only involves cutting a small piece off the ends of the stems if they become wet and soggy, but dipping the ends in varnish or polyurethane makes an excellent seal. It also means that you have to rearrange the dried flowers again when the fresh ones have died, and this ensures that you won't keep the same old collection gathering dust in a corner all winter.

One permanent dried group is effective as decoration in the house, but do remember to move it round to different positions so that you don't tire of seeing it always in the same place. An excellent group can be made from a mixture of some glycerined materials and some feathery dried seed heads, with the help of dried yarrow or hydrangea heads for added colour, and to give a good solid central point.

Principles and Methods. Even after all these years the arrangements that give me the greatest pleasure are the ones that I pick into my hand as I wander round my garden, often with a particular container in mind. This way I find that I don't pick things that are much too tall and then have to discard them or waste a good deal. The only exception comes when taking, for instance, low branches from a flowering tree (those planted in grass often get in the way of the grass cutter) in which case you should always take the branch back to the trunk, and later cut off the lengths you require. Apart from this, picking for a certain vase means that you will cut all material to the correct lengths and no time will be lost before you can condition it—and it is important to do this quickly to make everything last as long as possible.

Personal choice comes into the method you choose to hold the stems in the container—a pinholder, an Oasis-type block or wire netting. I still use a lot of chicken wire, but this may be because neither pinholders nor Oasis existed when I first started—it's all so long ago! I think you should use whichever method you find easiest. Pinholders are excellent for a few daffodils, but quite useless for mass arrangements, where wire is better. It is essential that a pinholder should be really firm, and you can fix it with either some very sticky fixative, or with plasticine: roll a piece of plasticine in your hands until you have a strip, make this into a circle to fit the base of the pinholder, and then press the pinholder with its plasticine base firmly into place in the container. Make sure that all the surfaces are dry or the plasticine will not stick.

I personally feel that chicken wire, or a combination of Oasis and wire, is essential for a table centre arrangement. It is necessary to have a build-up of wire netting to come to the top of the container, so that stems placed in the centre of the vase do not fall over, and those threaded through the wire horizontally are held with their stem ends in the water and yet flow gracefully over the lip of the container. As you will be sitting and looking at the arrangement, it is very important in this case that the flowers flow well over the edges of the vase, as otherwise you will be able to see all the mechanics.

For the upright urn-type of vase and arrangement, the tallest stem is the most important, for if this should slip, it will not only disarrange the whole vase, but is almost impossible to correct. So be sure to fix the main stem very firmly by whichever method you have chosen. This stem can be placed either to the right or left of the centre—I find that if it is off centre it will make the arrangement less stiffly symmetrical, with a result that will be more pleasing to the eye than if the whole is dead centre. Wherever you place it, the tallest stem must be absolutely vertical. The next stage is to fill in a roughly fan-shaped background, for which I suggest using lighter material. The pieces on either side should be slightly lower than the central stem. The guide on proportions is that the overall height of the arrangement should be one and a half to twice the height of the container, and the overall width should be about the same as the height. These are only rough figures, but I think that they are helpful.

Having achieved the outline shape with foliage or delicate flower sprays, then you add the central or focal point, made with an uneven number of flowers. Whenever possible I like to use flat-headed flowers or ones with many petals, such as open roses, dahlias or chrysanthemums, as these give a clear and distinctive central point where the eye focuses first. Two or three stems of these flowers should be placed so that their heads come well over the rim of the vase. Then place the next two well back, recessed so that they intensify the colour effect. It is interesting that the colour you place in the centre like this will dominate the vase, so if you have only three pink flowers and you want the vase to look really pink, then you must try to place these right in the middle.

Remember to place all stems in your arrangements so that they lead towards the middle of the vase. Look at each stem as you pick it, and try to choose pieces that will curve naturally either to the left or right. Then position them so that they fall gracefully from the edge of the container. Such subjects as ivy, Old Man's Beard, *Alchemilla mollis* and Solomon's Seal are good examples of stems that have a natural curve.

Try not to cut stems too short: by holding them against the vase, you can get a pretty good idea of how long you want them to be before you actually cut them. Once placed in position, it is best not to take them in and out too often, as this does prevent them living so long, for they hate constant handling.

Lastly, make sure that all the stems are well under the water line, especially those you have placed to flow out on either side; and it is always important to see that the vase is filled to the very top with water.

When making a simple arrangement, such as the one shown on page 122 in the shallow blue-grey oblong container, I used a pinholder, and cut the stems to different lengths so that they would all flow from the central point. I have grown to love these simple vases—they have a peaceful effect and are so pleasant to have in the house.

Green arrangements take a little longer to pick and condition, for they have to be more carefully thought out, and nicely contrasting shapes and colours of material chosen. Use some tall slender spiky leaf or branch for the outline of the vase—the different shapes of leaves are as important as the colours. In green arrangements I always like to use some kind of variegated foliage, for I feel this brings to the arrangement the same light touch that the growing plant provides in the garden. A different kind of colour contrast can be achieved by the use of grey material—leaves of artichoke, senecio or artemisia for instance. As with other arrangements the centre should be created by using a round leaf or rounded green head, such as allium, green zinnia or *Euphorbia polychroma* in spring. I think it is well worth taking the extra trouble involved in making green arrangements, for you can create something quite different almost every week as material from the garden changes, the finished effect is most attractive, and these groups last particularly well.

Different again are arrangements of flowers and unrelated foliage, and here colour plays an important part. It is fascinating to create vases with particular colour themes, either shades of one colour or providing contrasts. I love the simple effect of two-colour arrangements, and have suggested many in this book: green and white, green and blue, black and white, pink and grey and so on. A lovely colour contrast can be achieved by using dark grapes, reddish berberis and some red beetroot leaves with white roses, similar to the arrangement shown on page 131. Autumn is a marvellous time of year for creating vases of flowers and foliage that blend together: for instance, turning autumn leaves with apricot-coloured dahlias and roses and a stem of late lupin. Many other combinations are given under various plants in the earlier chapters.

Containers. I feel that I must add a few words about containers, as they play such a vital part in any flower arrangement. If you have only a few flowers, then the vase is very important indeed. If you have plenty of flowers and foliage to pick, then naturally the vase is of little consequence, as it can be hidden with either flowers or leaves.

There are many pretty flower vases on the market today, including little urns and white china figurines that are quite inexpensive. Choose a vase that looks well without too many flowers, and preferably not in too strong a colour, as this will limit its usefulness. I have collected containers of many kinds all over the world, and have a good collection of alabaster vases that I bought many moons ago.

Any deep dish or shallow urn raised on a stem make for easy arranging. This type of vase lifts up the flowers and gives a much more elegant-looking arrangement than the same material in a tumbler-shaped vase. I prefer shallow vases, but then I am quite prepared to fill them up all the time, and this is very important.

Crystal or glass vases look lovely when filled with something light and pretty such as gypsophila or old man's beard, and placed against the light so that you get an ethereal effect. The water must be crystal clear too, and a very little household bleach or chlorine added to it will help to keep it clean. Irises look good in glass and so do roses, especially if the stems are covered in thorn and you can see them through the glass.

Flowers seem to last best in metal vases, perhaps simply because the stems are kept cool: so bronze, copper or brass containers are all excellent. For a mass arrangement of all one type of flower you need a very plain container, and a box with a lid or a basket can be used most effectively. Your kitchen cupboard can yield some attractive containers: a sauce boat, soup bowl, decorated pyrex dish or pretty jug. Some of these can be seen in use among the illustrations to this book.

Conditioning. Although I have mentioned the best method of conditioning under each plant description, I would like to add a brief summary of this very important aspect of flower arranging.

When I started doing flowers, we were told to hammer all hardy and woody stems and cut all soft ones, and then give everything a long drink of warm water. Though this is still good advice today, we have learnt a great deal more about the movement of sap, and air bubbles that can prevent the cut stems from drinking freely, and so we now realize the value of burning or boiling the stem ends to help the flower to last much longer.

The method I would recommend is to place the ends of stems, as soon as possible after cutting, into a jug containing 1 in (2·5 cm) of really boiling water, count to twenty and then fill the jug up with cold water and leave the stems to drink for several hours, and preferably overnight. If the stems are tender, they should be allowed less time in the boiling water, if they are woody they can be allowed to stand in it for several minutes and no harm is done.

Poppies should be re-boiled if you have to cut the stems a second time; I try to cut and boil them at different lengths to avoid this. They are about the only flowers that do need to be re-boiled—most flowers only need to be treated once.

If you have a gas flame, you can burn the ends of the stems in that equally well. The Dutch and Japanese method of cutting the ends of the stems under water has the same effect of releasing the air bubble, and this can also be used successfully.

Calendar of Materials

In order that the lists should not be inordinately long, I have arranged the plants under the months in which they are in flower. In the case of foliage, which may be used a number of times throughout the year, I have listed the subject under the months in which I find it exceptionally useful.

January
Alnus (Alder)
Aralia
Aucuba japonica
Camellia
Cedrus atlantica 'Glauca'
Choisya ternata
Elaeagnus pungens
Eucalyptus
Euonymus
Garrya elliptica
Hedera (Ivy)
Jasminum (Jasmine)
Magnolia grandiflora
Mahonia
Viburnum

February
Alnus (Alder)
Aucuba japonica
Arum italicum
Bergenia
Camellia
Cedrus atlantica 'Glauca'
Chimonanthus (Winter Sweet)
Choisya ternata
Crocus
Elaeagnus pungens
Eranthis (Winter Aconite)

Eucalyptus
Euonymus
Galanthus (Snowdrop)
Garrya elliptica
Hedera (Ivy)
Helleborus—corsicus, foetidus, orientalis hybrids
Jasminum (Jasmine)
Magnolia grandiflora
Mahonia
Narcissus
Petasites
Prunus
Pulmonaria
Salix (Willow)
Viburnum

March
Alnus (Alder)
Aucuba japonica
Arum italicum
Bergenia
Camellia
Carpinus betulus (Hornbeam)
Cedrus atlantica 'Glauca'
Chimonanthus (Winter Sweet)
Chionodoxa
Choisya ternata
Corylus

Crocus
Cyclamen coum
Daphne mezereum
Elaeagnus pungens
Eranthis (Winter Aconite)
Erica carnea
Eucalyptus
Euonymus
Forsythia
Galanthus (Snowdrop)
Hamamelis mollis (Witch Hazel)
Hedera (Ivy)
Helleborus—corsicus, foetidus, orientalis hybrids
Jasminum (Jasmine)
Leucojum (Snowflake)
Magnolia grandiflora
Mahonia
Narcissus
Petasites
Primula
Prunus
Pulsatilla
Ribes
Rhododendron
Salix (Willow)
Viburnum
Zantedeschia

153

April
Acer (Maple)
Allium
Arum italicum
Bergenia
Camellia
Chimonanthus (Winter Sweet)
Cornus
Corylopsis
Cynara (Artichoke)
Daphne
Elaeagnus pungens
Erythronium
Forsythia
Fritillaria
Hedera (Ivy)
Helleborus—corsicus, foetidus,
   orientalis hybrids
Hyacinth
Magnolia grandiflora
Narcissus
Polygonatum (Solomon's Seal)
Prunus
Ranunculus
Rhododendron
Ribes
Salix (Willow)
Trollius
Tulip
Viburnum

May
Allium
Azalea
Camellia
Clematis
Convallaria majalis
   (Lily of the Valley)
Cornus kousa
Cynara (Artichoke)
Daphne
Dicentra
Dictamnus
Digitalis
Euphorbia
Hedera (Ivy)
Helleborus corsicus

Hemerocallis (Day Lily)
Hyacinth
Ligustrum
Lilac
Lonicera
Lupinus (Lupin)
Paeonia (Peony)
Prunus
Rheum
Rhododendron
Senecio
Tellima
Tiarella
Tulip
Wistaria

June
Alstroemeria
Angelica
Astrantia
Betula (Birch)
Campanula
Clematis
Cynara (Artichoke)
Delphinium
Dictamnus
Digitalis
Epimedium
Eryngium
Euphorbia
Geranium
Heuchera
Hosta
Iris
Ligustrum
Lilac
Lonicera
Lupinus (Lupin)
Macleaya
Nepeta
Onopordum
Paeonia (Peony)
Papaver (Poppy)
Penstemon
Polygonum
Prunella
Rosa (Rose)

Senecio
Smilacina
Thalictrum
Tiarella
Verbascum
Vinca
Yucca

July
Acanthus
Achillea
Aconitum
Alchemilla
Anaphalis
Angelica
Artemisia
Ballota
Betula (Birch)
Campanula
Crocosmia
Cynara (Artichoke)
Dahlia
Delphinium
Dianthus
Eryngium
Filipendula
Gentiana (Gentian)
Geranium
Gladiolus
Heuchera
Hosta
Kniphofia (Red Hot Poker)
Lavendula (Lavender)
Ligustrum
Lily
Macleaya
Nepeta
Onopordum
Paeonia (Peony)
Papaver (Poppy)
Penstemon
Philadelphus
Phlox
Phytolacca
Polygonum
Rosa (Rose)
Salvia

Scabiosa (Scabious)
Sedum
Sisyrinchium
Stachys lanata
Thalictrum
Verbascum
Yucca

August
Acanthus
Achillea
Agapanthus
Alchemilla
Amaranthus
Anaphalis
Angelica
Antirrhinum
Artemisia
Atriplex
Ballota
Buddleia
Campanula
Cobaea scandens
Cortaderia (Pampas Grass)
Crocosmia
Cynara (Artichoke)
Dahlia
Delphinium
Dianthus
Eryngium
Filipendula
Gentiana (Gentian)
Geranium
Gladiolus
Hosta
Hydrangea
Ligustrum
Lily
Macleaya
Moluccella
Nepeta
Nicotiana
Philadelphus
Phlox
Phytolacca
Rosa (Rose)
Rudbeckia

Scabiosa (Scabious)
Sedum
Sisyrinchium
Stachys lanata
Veratrum
Yucca
Zinnia

September
Acanthus
Agapanthus
Alchemilla
Amaranthus
Anemone
Artemisia
Calluna (Ling)
Carpinus betulus (Hornbeam)
Cobaea scandens
Cortaderia (Pampas Grass)
Cotinus
Dahlia
Gentiana (Gentian)
Geranium
Gladiolus
Hydrangea
Kniphofia (Red Hot Poker)
Lily
Nerine
Nicotiana
Phytolacca
Rosa (Rose)
Sedum
Zinnia

October
Agapanthus
Ampelopsis (Virginia Creeper)
Arbutus
Artemisia
Berberis
Celastrus (Bitter-sweet)
Cimicifuga
Cobaea scandens
Colchicum
Cortaderia (Pampas Grass)
Cotoneaster
Cyclamen neapolitanum

Dahlia
Epimedium
Fagus (Beech)
Forsythia
Gentiana (Gentian)
Gladiolus
Hydrangea
Nerine
Osmunda
Pernettya
Phytolacca
Pyracantha
Rodgersia
Rosa (Rose)
Scrophularia
Sedum
Symphoricarpus (Snowberry)
Vitis

November
Berberis
Cedrus atlantica 'Glauca'
Chrysanthemum
Cotoneaster
Elaeagnus
Euonymus
Hedera (Ivy)
Pachysandra
Viburnum

December
Alnus (Alder)
Aralia
Bergenia
Cedrus atlantica 'Glauca'
Cotoneaster
Elaeagnus
Euonymus
Garrya elliptica
Hedera (Ivy)
Helleborus niger
Magnolia grandiflora
Mahonia
Pachysandra
Viburnum

Climate Zones

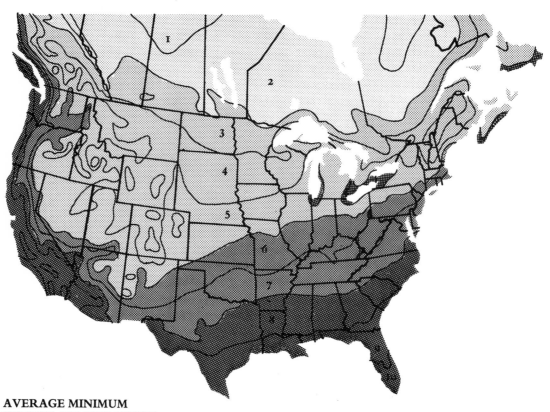

**AVERAGE MINIMUM
WINTER TEMPERATURE**

Zones 1 and 2,
below —40°

Zones 3, 4 and 5,
—10° to —40°

Zones 6 and 7, 10°
to —10°

Zones 8, 9 and 10,
40° to 10°

Index